ONE
School
NOW

Studies in the
Postmodern Theory of Education

Joe L. Kincheloe and Shirley R. Steinberg
General Editors

Vol. 52

PETER LANG
New York • Washington, D.C./Baltimore • Boston
Bern • Frankfurt am Main • Berlin • Vienna • Paris

Peter S. Temes

ONE
School
NOW

Real Life at Lynn English High

PETER LANG
New York • Washington, D.C./Baltimore • Boston
Bern • Frankfurt am Main • Berlin • Vienna • Paris

Library of Congress Cataloging-in-Publication Data

Temes, Peter S.
One school now: real life at Lynn English High / Peter S. Temes.
p. cm. — (Counterpoints; 52)
Includes bibliographical references (p.   ).
1. Discrimination in education—Massachusetts—Lynn—Case studies.
2. Minority youth—Education (Secondary)—Massachusetts—Lynn—Case
studies. 3. High schools—Massachusetts—Lynn—Case studies.
4. Lynn English High School (Lynn, Mass.). I. Title. II. Series:
Counterpoints (New York, N.Y.); vol. 52.
LC212.23.L96T46   373.744'5—dc21   97-11730
ISBN 0-8204-3746-8
ISSN 1058-1634

Die Deutsche Bibliothek-CIP-Einheitsaufnahme

Temes, Peter S.:
One school now: real life at Lynn English High / Peter S. Temes.
–New York; Washington, D.C./Baltimore; Boston; Bern;
Frankfurt am Main; Berlin; Vienna; Paris: Lang.
(Counterpoints; 52)
ISBN 0-8204-3746-8

Cover design by James F. Brisson.

The paper in this book meets the guidelines for permanence and durability
of the Committee on Production Guidelines for Book Longevity
of the Council of Library Resources.

Printed in the United States of America.

Contents

Introduction

A few years ago, I was sitting in the new home of a man who had once been a teaching colleague of mine in New York City. He had moved to a small town in Pennsylvania, about two hundred miles from New York. Those two hundred miles meant a kind of safety to this man, a distance from the dangers and complications of big city life. His new town was, in his eyes, something quite different: a calm place. But every now and then, even rural Pennsylvania let him down.

A television was on somewhere that day—not in the living room, where we were, but close by, maybe in the dining room, maybe the kitchen. We heard a news announcer say that the county fairgrounds had been the scene of a break-in earlier that afternoon. Windows had been smashed, money stolen from concession stands. My colleague happened to catch a glimpse of the television about then, and all of a sudden he started stomping his foot, calling out "I knew it! I knew it!" On the screen, a dark-skinned man was talking about what he had seen at the ransacked fairgrounds, the word "witness" superimposed in white across the lower part of the picture.

I was startled. What had my colleague known? That the witness to this crime was black? Clearly not. I guessed that he saw the dark face and then assumed that this fellow was somehow a part of the crime. What a racist, I thought, and that's still what I think. But he was saying something important, however ugly it might also have been. He was saying that in his mind, when bad things happen, black people can't be too far away. And that, I'm sure, is one reason he had left New York City—to get away from black people.

When I began writing the pages that follow, I didn't think that I was writing about race or racism. I thought I was writing about education—more specifically, I thought I was writing the story of one school not far from where I live. But in fact race is the central story of this book, just as it is the central story of public education in America today.

In the months I spent sitting in on classes, talking with students and with teachers, the question of race was almost never spoken about directly, but it was always present. The great scholar W.E.B. Du Bois described the situation perfectly in his 1903 book *The Souls of Black Folk*. "Between me and the other world," wrote Du Bois, the first African American to earn a Ph.D. from Harvard, "there is ever an unasked question: unasked by some through feelings of delicacy; by others through the difficulty of rightly framing it. All, nevertheless, flutter round it. . . . To the real question, How does it feel to be a problem? I answer seldom a word."

My colleague's mind was probably full of unasked questions, too. The obvious question on his mind—how can I get away from these people—was, I think, obscuring a more important one: why aren't they more like us?

And this is the giant question about education in America that everyone seems to flutter around but never ask directly: why aren't black and Hispanic students more like white students? Other questions follow from it: Why aren't they performing as well? Why aren't they grateful to their teachers? Why is teaching them so much harder than teaching white students? These questions might seem unfair, or even grotesque, but they are common questions in the minds of the teachers I met at the school I studied and in other schools around the country.

And these questions have answers.

First, nonwhite students *are* like us, if "us" means Americans generally. My colleague in Pennsylvania saw on television a black man who witnessed a crime. He saw a citizen, not a criminal. He saw a man very much like himself, but he failed to recognize that fact. In American schools, the same thing often happens. A teacher hears a student laughing and joking with friends in a language he doesn't speak, and instead of recognizing that he is seeing something normal, something joyful, he often feels that he is seeing something mysterious or even scary. One teacher you will read about in this book expelled a student from her class, and then saw him in the hall, talking with his friends in Spanish, and laughing. The teacher doesn't speak Spanish, but she was sure her student and his friends were talking about her, laughing at her.

Another question: Why don't nonwhite students perform as well as white students? In the school I visited, two answers became clear. First, nonwhite students came from more dangerous parts of town, and seemed to have less support for their education at home. But this observation, true to the point of being a truism, a cliché, is painfully incomplete. In fact, African American and Hispanic students at the school I visited *did* perform as well at the tasks they were given as most white students perform at their tasks, but this is hard to see *because they were generally given different tasks.* Black and Hispanic students were generally placed in different classes from white students, were often encouraged by teachers, coaches, and school administrators to spend more time working at sports than at academics, and were asked more often to be peaceful than to be smart.

These observations will sound harsh to many, particularly to white teachers teaching at schools with many African American and Hispanic students. But these teachers understand what is going on; they see how differently African American, Hispanic and white students are treated. Most of these teachers feel trapped: they don't *want* to offer different standards and different expectations based on race, yet they feel they have no choice. One woman who had been teaching reading for ten years told me that she tried to treat all her students with equal respect, but that she felt it was impossible: "Here they come in the morning, five kids, ten kids, all at different levels. When I work with them, I teach every one of them what I think they are ready to learn. If I look at them as a group, the white kids are ready to learn the most, the blacks are not ready at all. I wouldn't make this up. My job would be easier if these kids could all do the same work, if they all came to me with the same background." Another, a man with only three years of teaching experience, explains why he expects different things from his white students than from his black students: "I love these kids. That's why I'm teaching. I want them to come in here and become the best thinkers and doers they can be. My subject is science, and they all learn science. But I can't say to a student who can't add that he's ready for chemistry. And I can't say to a student who's going to Princeton next year that he's got to work only up to average standards. So different students wind up doing different work. My honors classes, they work at college level already. Yes, they're almost all white. And my basic level classes, they still need to talk about the basic concepts—what is scientific method, what kinds of questions can science answer. They're lucky if they can really think in terms of why the periodic table of elements is a valuable tool. But can they work with the table—the basic kids, on the noncollege track? No. And I can't pretend they can." And these students, these "basic" students, are almost all African American and Hispanic.

These teachers feel uneasy, but see no way out of the system of separation they gently enforce.

What can be done? Judging from the many school reform projects abroad in the land today, a good deal. But judging from the measures of contentment and performance of students—not to mention the consistent degree of racial segregation in American schools—not much of it is really helping. Looking back over a year inside one high school, I found myself thinking a surprising thought: How much or how little help the systems and authorities of schools offer their students isn't really that important. The students themselves are such strong creatures, that with very little help at all they can learn tremendously well. It is far more important for schools to follow the physician's ancient code, *first, do no harm*, than to worry as much as we do about the ways of *helping*. A good school, I'm now convinced, does its best work by getting out of a student's way. The few tasks a school needs to do well are indeed vital—they involve things like encouraging students to pay attention to their own best talents and interests, and helping them find ways to connect those talents and interests to the work of the world at large. But these tasks are few.

Some of the lessons that students learn in most schools are really terrible: at the top of the list is the lesson that money is the root of security in life. Again and again, teachers tell bored students to pay attention so that they can do well in school, and get a good job one day. "Where will you be without an education?" one teacher I met asked his students frequently.

"I'll tell you where," he'd continue. "In the streets, no job, no money, nothing. So stick it out." Many of the marginal students I got to know heard this and took it to heart. Their inner compasses set toward the magnetic North of money, these kids sooner or later realize that they aren't learning what they are expected to learn no matter hard they try, and they turn with some frequency to the other ways of following their teacher's advice about the importance of money. At the school I visited, "making money" is slang for dealing drugs. So I wonder, what lesson is this good-hearted teacher teaching? From his perspective and in terms of the experience of his own life, his advice makes perfect sense. But in terms of the experiences of his students, his advice is all wrong: it cultivates desires that many cannot meaningfully fulfill for themselves.

The students you will read about in this book fall easily into two categories—those whose schooling is preparing them for the social and professional opportunities they will have in their lives, and those whose educations are misleading them.

The students in the first group are mostly white. The students in the second group are mostly black. What amazes me is that the students who aren't being well prepared for their work lives keep coming back to school. This is probably the biggest difference in American schools today compared to even one generation ago.

Just the other day, I heard on the news that the high school my grandfather attended in the 1930s had been closed as part of a program in New York City to shut down schools that were graduating fewer than forty percent of their students. Isn't it incredible, I said to a friend, that today you can have a school where more students fail than succeed? Then I remembered that my grandfather hadn't graduated either, and that most of his peers, the sons and daughters of newly-arrived immigrants, also left school before graduating. They left school to work, usually miserable jobs, but through those jobs they built reasonable if difficult lives for themselves and their families. Today, that is less likely to happen. Today, there are few jobs at all for high school dropouts, and virtually none that can even begin to support a family.

That fact makes dropping out harder today. There are fewer alternatives to school, so many students stick it out even though they get little from the ritual of showing up in the morning and going back home at the end of the day. Many leave school every afternoon no smarter, no happier, and with little more hope, and yet they keep returning. They have been fooled. Fooled by the social message coming to them from television, from the movies, from their heroes: stay in school. But schools give them precious little. Many, many teachers I met would be happier if the hardest cases just stopped coming. Let them go out and work instead, except that there are no jobs for them. Let them mature a bit before they come back to school, except that the lessons they'll learn on the streets will make them even less likely to succeed in the long run.

So what is the answer? Here's my two cents' worth, based on my close-up look at one tough-luck school: make school more meaningful for the most challenging students by demanding of them that they work very hard at the things they already know how to do. Then tie those things they already know how to do back into a curriculum of skills that will help them have meaningful social lives and work lives once their schooling ends. Why do I think this can work? Because even the most at-risk students tend to try hard to do what we ask them to do. If we ask them to do things they can't do at all, they'll try, fail, and give up. If we ask them to do challenging things within their abilities, they'll succeed, and then we can have them try progressively harder and more intellectually meaningful things.

(On my bookshelf I find John Dewey's small volume, *The School and Society*, from 1900. In it he writes about how the typical young person "is already running over, spilling over, with activities of all kinds. He is not a purely latent being whom the adult has to approach with great caution and skill in order gradually to draw out some hidden germ of activity. . . . The question of education is the question of taking hold of his activities, of giving them direction. Through direction, through organized use, they tend toward valuable results, instead of scattering or being left to merely impulsive expression.")

An example: in this book you will meet a young black man named Jay who does very poorly in his classes, but excels in playing basketball and football. He plays these games because the school makes it possible to play them—he says as much himself. He's on the school teams, though he worries he'll get thrown off for low grades (he had to repeat tenth grade because he failed all his classes the first time around.) He throws his entire spirit and much of his intellect into playing ball—he simply couldn't play ball as well as he does without doing that. And then the games end, the seasons end, and he goes back to the misery of his classes. No one connects the two for him. He does not learn the angles and trajectories of his freethrow attempts, or the social history of football. He doesn't know the history of baseball's Negro League, and he knows few of the lessons of American history and civics that the story of the Negro League brings into high relief. He demonstrates through his discipline in sports that he can listen, that he can work hard, that he can learn. And no one finds a way to funnel the power of mind and spirit evident on the ballfield toward the classroom. That is a tragedy, and no one can miss the fact that this young man is black, and the teachers who fail him are white.

Race is not the cause of Jay's poor performance or of his teachers' neglect, but race lets us off the hook. Like my colleague in Pennsylvania, we stand in our rooms and say, "I knew it," while in fact we don't know very much at all. We particularly don't seem to know how to save ourselves from our own failed attempts to share the good things in our lives with the young people who come to school because we ask them to.

There are in this book several white people who are fine teachers and administrators—I would even say some, like the principal you will meet here, are gifted. They work hard and solve difficult problems, but they do not begin to untie the knot of race that complicates their lives so deeply, and which they almost never speak of.

And then there is one white man who, while speaking seldom about race, does what sometimes seems impossible: he overcomes it. He is my hero, the hero of this book, though I went looking for none. In fact I had hoped that if I did by chance find a hero, he or she would look different, be from someplace more interesting, and bear more of a resemblance either to his or her students, or to me.

But this man is white, is a local, did not study at a notable college or university, and dislikes the language of school reform. What he does is love and respect his students with unusual power. I knew I had found a rare teacher when he said to me one day, "I'd like to teach these kids spiritualism. I'd like to take them mountain climbing."

At that moment I knew he could make the intuitive connections between hopes (teaching them spiritualism) and acts (taking them mountain climbing), and between what he knows they can do (work with their bodies) and what he as a teacher must direct them to learn (develop their minds and spirits). Another passage from Dewey's turn-of-the-century book explains exactly what this extraordinary teacher is doing. Dewey is writing here about "the occupation," and he means occupations in general, the things that young people do simply because they like doing them. "The occupation," Dewey writes, "supplies the child with a genuine motive; it gives him experience at first hand; it brings him into contact with realities. It does all this, but in addition it is liberalized by translation into its historic and social values and scientific equivalencies. With the growth of the child's mind in power and knowledge it ceases to be a pleasant occupation merely and becomes more and more a medium, an instrument, an organ of understanding." So if the teacher takes a thing a student already does, and turns it toward some lessons about how the thing is done, who did it first, the principles of history and math and science involved in the doing, then the teacher helps the student live a more thoughtful life. Then education is happening.

If the teacher I so admire is different from most others, that difference lies in his faith in his students. He realizes that they have all the capacity for wonder and for deep feeling that he has. He wants only for them to trust him enough to bring that capacity out in the open, so he can build upon it, turn it toward the lessons of life that they desperately need, even if they don't yet understand their own needs for education. If he must take them up a mountain for them to offer him their hearts, he is ready.

He gives me hope about his school, and schools in America generally. The students you will meet in these pages give me even more hope. For all the difficulty and even tragedy in this book, it is a book about youth and therefore it is at its center a romance, foretelling good things.

When we see schools without hope, we must recognize that we are looking at schools where students do not play a big enough role in the work of their own lives. In these schools, we must ask the students how we can help them, and we must listen. The school I visited is run by an energetic man who has made many good changes in his short time as principal. He has helped the school become safer and more orderly. These changes are part of his deep desire to have his school seem as good to its students and to the world as the suburban schools he had known as a student, teacher, and coach. But as he looks toward his ideal, his model, he necessarily looks away from the unexpected grace and talents in even his most troublesome students.

Not far from this school, about one hundred years before it was built, Ralph Waldo Emerson said this about the problem of following models too closely: "Let me admonish you, first of all, to go alone, to refuse the good models, even those which are sacred in the imagination of men. . . . Imitation cannot go above its model. The imitator dooms himself to hopeless mediocrity. The inventor did it because it was natural to him, and so in him it has a charm. In the imitator something else is natural, and he bereaves himself of his own beauty, to come short of another man's." The students I met in my work on this book generally fall short of other men's measures. But they are geniuses in living their own lives. If we ask them to be only well behaved, to be only normal, their genius is dead to us; it will not let us help them save themselves from the poverty and isolation of the uneducated in America today.

White men and women cannot save failing schools. Nor can black men and women, nor can any other teachers and administrators. The students themselves are the only engines of change; in them are intricate models of change and hope and brilliance. The best teachers in this book hear them, and draw out their passions to live life well.

This book does not offer any programs or many-pointed plans for "reengineering" our schools. Instead it offers the voices of students, so we may hear their genius. "The true romance which the world exists to realize," Emerson wrote in 1844, as he looked out over a disunited nation full of vast but untapped talents, "will be the transformation of genius into practical power." This seems to me not too ambitious a task for our schools as well.

Chapter One

Lynn, Lynn

"Lynn, Lynn, city of sin."

Lynners hate that little rhyme. It reminds them that among the handful of quiet suburban towns that make up the Boston area's North Shore, Lynn is feared. The prosperous professionals who pay two and three hundred thousand dollars for homes in places like Marblehead and Swampscott aren't amused either; the rhyme reminds them that no one is ever far from poverty and crime.

It's pretty much the same for blue-collar refugees from Boston, too. As the old city neighborhoods like Dorchester and Mattapan began turning from white to black and brown, lots of Boston's white ethnic tradesmen, shopkeepers, and clerical workers saved up and bought into the North Shore's less expensive towns, towns like Danvers and Peabody. But they hear that little rhyme, "Lynn, Lynn, city of sin," and they become a little nervous, because Lynn lies right in the center of the North Shore. Half the places they want to go, they'll have to get there by driving through the city of sin.

Or, instead of driving, they could take the commuter train down to Boston. But even then they'll stop and wait for passengers to board at the new central depot in Lynn, a ten-million dollar renovation that looks great, but remains mostly unused. The train waits in Lynn, but generally no one gets on; the station's almost always empty. The shops on the lower level were never rented out, and half their storefronts are already covered by graffiti. Dressed for work, looking out the commuter train window, who doesn't wonder what goes on there at night? The newspaper offers some suggestions with occasional stories about crackdowns on prostitution, about drug busts, even murder.

Town boosters hate the rhyme enough that they've built an ad campaign around it. "Lynn, Lynn," read the billboards along the highway up from Logan airport, "city of firsts." First jet engine in the United States. First advertising firm. First air-mail drop. Most of the firsts have to do with General Electric, which was born in Lynn and drove the economy for decades. For years, though, G.E. has been laying off workers. In 1980 G.E. employed about 15,000 people in Lynn. In 1994, only about 5,000 jobs remained. In the end, the "firsts" campaign didn't do much good. Mostly it just reminded everyone of Lynn's faded glory, just as the cluster of mansions along Lynn's oceanfront reminds people of the town's lost wealth. Yet most of the mansions are still kept up. Some are funeral homes, some are rooming houses, and some still house old Lynn families without the wealth to reestablish themselves in grand houses elsewhere. More than a few have been bought by young couples who couldn't afford anything equally large in Swampscott, just to the north, or Marblehead, even pricier, one hop further up the coast. Still, though, most young couples looking to settle north of Boston don't even consider Lynn. The big worry, the word uttered in minivans tooling up the shore on househunting trips, is not "crime" (though crime *is* an issue) but "schools."

"A lot of Lynn is really lovely, especially near the water," says the mother of three young children in Marblehead. An architect, she sees the potential in the underpriced old New England homes in Lynn. "But, my God, could I see my kids in school there? I don't think so. Marblehead is a beautiful place—the beaches, the shore—but it's boring socially. Every other woman I meet here is married to a doctor or a lawyer and spends her day at exercise class. I'd like to live in Lynn, to spend less money, to live with a real range of people. But if I sent my kids off to those schools every day, then every day I'd feel like I was failing as a parent."

Evan is a student at Lynn English High School, though he didn't grow up in Lynn. He lived nearby, in Peabody, until his parents divorced. Then he and his mother moved into a relative's house in Lynn, right after he finished seventh grade.

For eighth grade, Evan walked two miles each morning to catch the bus to his middle school in Peabody—no one told the school that Evan had moved, and he felt safer staying with his old friends. The next year, he began English High, and the first week he was there he saw a girl stabbed in the chest with a scissor in front of the principal's office. His mother began to worry when he came home one day with the words "Fuck You" written across the back of his shirt, courtesy of the boy who sat behind him in homeroom. Many of his high school classes were less challenging than his work had been in middle school, but his grades went down anyway. He felt unsafe. The boy behind him in homeroom continued to harass Evan, and one day Evan snapped. He turned, screamed, and threw the boy across the room.

Things got better for Evan after that morning. A new principal came to English High, and the school became safer. Then Evan found a love for video and television production. He managed to lure donations of high-quality video equipment to the school, mostly through an internship with the local cable television company that a teacher had arranged for him. Now in his senior year, he produces a live news show at school every morning. Evan is obviously smart, but his grades still don't reflect his ability. High school in Peabody probably would have served him better academically. But he has a quiet kind of toughness that Peabody would never have given him.

I met Evan, who is white, when Grady, a black student at Lynn English, introduced me. If Grady reached out to put his hand on the average white kid from Peabody, that kid would pee in his pants. But as Grady told me "you should talk to this guy," he smacked Evan on the shoulder and smiled. Evan smiled, too. They made a surprising pair, standing together in a high school hallway: Evan is neat, a little nerdy, holding some spooled-up video cable in his hand, busily occupied with his after-school project; Grady is hip-hop baggy, the hood to his puffy black leather jacket pulled over his head. They are friends, though outside of school they never see each other.

Lynn English High School is a long low building of white brick and stone with a colonnade and neoclassical columns leading to its front doors. The doors are painted a bright red, and they clash with every other aspect of the sedate, sixty-year-old building. But the overall effect is still striking: Lynn English High School is a building with grace, surrounded by wide lawns and a long, curving driveway that makes you think of a Southern manor house. Inside, panes of glass in hallway doors are missing. The student bathrooms are full of cracked porcelain and black garbage bags are taped over unrepaired stalls. Classrooms overflow with mismatched furniture. Heavy oak chairs tucked under bright Formica desks stand beside blue plastic and steel desk-and-chair-in-one sets. It all feels like a haphazard collection of used kitchen furniture. But there is order in these rooms; not two hours after the students have gone for the day, custodians have straightened every chair and every desk, and the hallways of Lynn English are always well swept. The school's age, its wide, familiar hallways, the dark wood molding around every window and every door, and even the vague smell of cafeteria food all combine to suggest the mythical golden age of American high schools when teachers taught, students studied, and everyone looked more or less alike.

The students at English today look like a lot of things, but they do not look alike. In the last fifteen years, diversity has hit the school in a big way, and white students are just at the point of becoming a minority. Sitting with two students in the otherwise empty cafeteria at the end of a school day, it's not hard to see why the school, like the town, scares some people. But it's easy, too, to see how unfair that fear is, how it rejects the manifold worth of the young people in schools like English High, young people like Sandy and Jay.

Sandy is a year older than his cousin Jay. Sandy is taller, and built wider. His skin is very dark. He wears a young man's beard, not yet filled in, spotty. Jay is smaller, but not small. He smiles more, but is more shy.

Sandy looks directly at people passing by, almost challenging them, while Jay looks away. Sandy fits that terrible lurking image of the scruffy black man—unkempt, undisciplined, capable of anything. Jay is more stylish, just as baggy and hip-hop as his cousin, but neater.

The first time I met Sandy he was talking in the cafeteria with two of his friends. (Jay wasn't at school that day; later on I learned that he often wasn't.) Sandy sat across from a young woman with a full lunch tray who kept at her food; she didn't say a word. Next to Sandy was Joe, who looked a little old to be a student. In fact, he was a teacher's aide, which actually meant that he went to classes with a boy in a wheelchair, carrying his books, walking him from room to room. He'd graduated from Lynn's other high school, Lynn Classical, just a few months ago.

Sandy seemed shy, but he wanted to talk. "Well," he said, "this school, you know, it's not as bad as some people think it is. It's not that bad. It's all right. The teachers, they want you to work and all, but you know the problem? They just give it to you one time, you know—you get it the first time or you don't get it at all. You know what I'm saying?" Just then a large teacher—he turned out to be the soccer coach—sauntered over. He wanted to talk, too—about how the school used to be more orderly. But times changed. The students today are capable of behaving well, he said, but the leadership here is lax. The rules aren't followed enough. Tell a kid to take off his hat, he takes it off, turns the corner, and it's right back on again. Take a kid to the office, he gets a slap on the wrist. You practically have to kill someone to get suspended now, and kids walk around all the time wearing hats.

"Things are different, it's true," Sandy said. The coach looked surprised by the comment, thought about it for a moment, and then said, "Sandy doesn't know about that. How could he?" The coach had been at English High more than twenty years. He explained the changes he had seen over those years, having to do mostly with discipline, home life, and hat-wearing in the halls.

Sandy talked about sports a little. He played football and basketball. He was planning to go to a junior college in New York State next year, and he'd play football there too. He did all right in his classes, Bs and Cs, but, he said, "I'm not a real smart guy."

Having said that, he was quiet, and seemed to be thinking over what he had said. Was it really true? Then the coach said, "Sandy's street-smart. He's the smartest guy on the street, right Sandy?" The coach smiled. Sandy smiled too, and looked down. Then the coach took a turn to talk about sports. English had some good teams, he said, especially the soccer team. It was different from the other teams, the coach was saying. Soccer players got higher grades. "They're a different breed of kid." At that, Sandy raised his head for quick second, but then dropped it low again, and nodded mildly. A bell rang.

Two days later I sat with Sandy in the cafeteria after school. He was talking about the last time the police had come to English High, a few months ago. On a Friday night, he said, a black English student and two of his friends beat up a Hispanic student on a street corner in town, away from the school. The following Monday, the Hispanic student didn't show up at school, but he and about a dozen of his friends walked up to the main entrance a little after 2:30, dismissal time, and joined in the swarm of students walking out of the building into a warm autumn afternoon. One of the black students was walking toward a waiting school bus, right in front of the principal's office windows. The student who had been jumped was bigger than the student walking toward the bus. He stepped in his way, said something, and gave a high shove. The black student took a swing. "It was one-on-one," Sandy says, "then real quick it was three-on-one—the Spanish kid's friends started moving in, and they knocked the black kid down and kept on hitting at him and kicking at him. Then somebody had a golf club and wham! they hit him with that, but just once. The teachers, they all were at the office window, watching and pointing, but nobody came out till the cops came. But the kid was all right. He got up. He walked away."

Sitting in the cafeteria with Sandy, I also heard about a friend of his who had just been arrested. "For house invasion, with a gun. He's in lock-up now, though; they got him good. But he was a good guy. Everybody loved him because he was a good basketball player and he treated you all right, he didn't start trouble with people. But he spun out with the drugs, you know? They got into his head—he changed. Then he did some robberies, robbed some stores. I saw him fight sometimes—that's how you know he's having some trouble, because he was a rough kid, but he didn't used to get pleasure from hurting people. If someone got him mad, he would fight and then it would be over. But something changed in his head, and then when he would fight you just couldn't stop him. He didn't just want to win, he wanted to hurt you. Now, I get in some fights, but I can walk away, you know?

"My friend, he couldn't leave it alone. Nobody could stop him. He hits you, he wants to see you there bleeding. Before he got put away, he started walking around with a pistol. He'd say, 'Nobody can stop me now.' He really wanted to hurt people. So he's put away now, he's locked up." Sandy shakes his head, sorry even to think about this fact.

"But then, sometimes, I'd be thinking too, if I had a gun, what would I do? Maybe that's rubbing off on me. Nobody could stop me either."

People drift in and out of the cafeteria, some of them on their way to practice in the upstairs gym, some of them just killing time, not wanting to go home even though the school day has been over for an hour. But mostly Sandy and I are alone with a few hundred chairs and rows of long tables. Then Sandy smiles over at someone walking by, says hi, and his friend keeps going. As we continue to talk, Sandy gestures over my shoulder, but no one's there. He does it again, and then his friend peeks out of a doorway, trying to figure whether Sandy's in some kind of trouble. He's Jay, Sandy's younger cousin.

Jay really doesn't want to talk; he's too shy, and looks off into the distance, chuckling, shaking his head. In short nervous spurts he tells me he's in tenth grade, he gets As and Bs and Cs, he missed school for a while last year but this year he's playing basketball and coming around steadily. He doesn't want to talk about why he missed school last year.

Jay spends a lot of his time thinking about the future, he says. In a few years, he hopes to be playing professional ball. If he doesn't make it? "I don't know, man." He chuckles and looks down at his shoes, shaking his head. "Maybe a pimp," he says, and comes up grinning at Sandy and sees him laughing too. But Jay's a serious young man, smart, and while quick to laugh, he has a morbid side. "I'm different from other people," he says. "Other people, they're always joking. Not me." He's careful with his language. He seems less threatening than his cousin Sandy, more like a shy scholarship kid at a private school.

Jay says goodbye and says maybe he'll talk to me again later, but maybe not. "I don't know," he says, and then he's gone. Sandy turns back to the fight—the beating, really—in front of the principal's office in the fall, but he's not really saying much. It takes me a moment to figure out that Sandy doesn't want to talk about that; he wants to talk about Jay. Once Jay's been gone a minute—once Sandy's sure he's out of earshot—Sandy says, "That kid, man, he's not going to be straight with you. He's been through it, you know? He's done things I still can't hardly believe. I know he's got guns at his house—he's showed them to me, and he likes those pistols, boy, you can see that when he shows them to you. His mother don't really care— she's not on drugs or anything, but you know, she's not out there for him. He's got trouble coming. Last year, he missed school? He was in lock-up, DYS [Department of Youth Services]. Man, even last week, for the weekend, he was locked up." He stops for a minute, not happy to be telling this story. Then he continues: "Last year? He had an uncle who worked in the school, a teacher's aide like that guy with me before. He was fighting with Jay, Jay went into his backpack and took out a gun. Chased him down the street."

Sandy is the only one of Jay's friends at English High to see serious trouble looming in front of Jay. Everyone else I speak with says the same thing—"Jay's a good kid"—suggesting that his goodness alone will save him. They say that his problem is with the bad kids he hangs around with, it's not really about *him*. They seem to accept the idea that really bad things are only done by really bad people, not by kids who try to do right. It's a seductive notion. Could these kids, these boys any adult could sit and talk with, laugh with, coax out of their shyness— could they rob, beat, shoot? Only Sandy seems to realize that a kid with a good heart might still do the worst deeds. The others take too seriously all the emphasis at school—and other places—on looking nice, showing the world a calm face, and being seen in the right company. Sandy, on the other hand, says that sometimes he hangs out with "guys who rob and rape." He feels like he's a good influence on them, and he likes the thrill of their company, but he says he always walks away from real trouble. ("Once," he says, "there were five of us. One had a gun he just got that day, one had a knife. The one with the knife said, 'Let's go do a robbery.' The one with the gun said no, so he said, 'Then give up the gun, man, give it to me.' He was gonna, but I told him no, told him to forget about this guy just looking for trouble, and we walked away from it. That was my influence.") Sandy also chooses to look scruffy, sometimes even scary. He gives everyone the chance to misjudge him, because he is so sure of his own decency.

David is the boy who was clubbed in front of school. He's also a cousin, though a distant one, of Sandy and Jay. David has seen the trouble Jay's been in, but he thinks Jay is safe now. "He used to hang around with some bad people, but he hangs around with me now. His grades are getting higher. He's over that other shit now." I ask David if he can think of anyone at school who might be in serious trouble two or three years from now. He thinks a long time, then says "no, not really. These guys are all all right." But Sandy feels differently. He's worried about Jay. "He's on the edge, I know it. He's just balancing right now, better than he used to be, but not in a good place. I'm thinking about him all the time. Will he do all right? Will he be in jail again? I saw him over the weekend with some bad kids. Did he have a pistol with him? I don't know. Did some of those guys he was with have a pistol? No question about it.

"I'm thinking he's gonna fall over the edge. He's maybe gonna beat on somebody at school, or go steal something and get caught, and then they'll throw him out of school. When that happens, that's it, nothing else'll keep him on the straight track, he'll go over to the other side, rob and steal all day, get high, burn up. That'll be the end. I worry about it. I think maybe it's coming soon for him. His mother don't care. Some people in my family say she's no good, she's a crackhead. Now I don't know if this is really true so I say it's not, but do I know really? No, I don't. I do know his apartment is small and ugly. His street is a bad street, over in West Lynn, with the triple deckers and all? There's some empty houses on his street, some of them are crackhouses sometimes. Not every day, but if the man is in, you know what I mean? If the man is in that day, then it's a crackhouse that day.

"I'm keeping my eye on Jay. This month, next month, if he's staying straight, then maybe he'll be all right. So I'm looking out every day. I can't stop him if he wants to be on the hard side, but I want to know about it. That's all. I just want to know if he's doing right or not, if he's still got a chance to come out and live to be a old man, you know? I'm just keeping my eye on him for that."

Sandy's story about Jay chasing his uncle down the street was true. I had already heard it from Joe Patuleia, the principal, while we watched a basketball practice together. Patuleia takes real pride in the athletic power of some of his students. As we watched the practice, I asked him how many of the kids on the team would wind up graduating. "These kids? Oh, they'll graduate," he said. All of them? "Yeah, I think so." He thought some more. "That kid there? Near the hoop? We almost had to have him arrested. Last year his uncle worked here, and he chased him down the street with a gun." Patuleia still seemed surprised by this fact, and it *was* surprising that this quiet-looking kid could be there waiting patiently for his turn to run drills, and last year, or last week, or maybe tomorrow, he could be running after someone with pistol, ready to kill a man in the street. "He's a hell of a ballplayer," Patuleia said. "I think he'll graduate."

Joe Patuleia had been a math teacher and basketball coach at a white suburban high school for sixteen years before coming to English a year-and-a-half ago. Grandson of Portuguese immigrants, Patuleia was an unusually happy teacher—he loved being in the classroom, loved being on the sports field, loved spending time with his students. His ambition was to be a great teacher and a great coach, and for a number of years he lived a perfectly fulfilled professional life: he *was* precisely what he wanted to be. Then, about five years ago, something changed for Patuleia. He began to believe that he had a different role to play. He started taking graduate classes at Harvard, and he did well. He liked the ideas he encountered there. He like the larger scale of thinking, the bigger questions and bigger challenges. Soon enough, he decided that he wanted to be a principal.

After taking a sabbatical to finish his master's degree at Harvard, Patuleia left the security of his teaching and coaching job in the western suburbs for a vice-principalship in Manchester-by-the-Sea, a tony shoreline community on the north coast. A year later, the school reorganized, and his job was cut. Suddenly, after success at Harvard, after success as a vice-principal, he had no job at all. Scrambling, he found a new position as principal of a small high school in New Hampshire, but he knew going in that it wouldn't last long. He wanted to be near Boston. He didn't like the rural life, and he didn't want to be forgotten in a small village school. So he continued to look for a principalship closer to home, and soon he found one, at Lynn English High.

"I wasn't sure I wanted this job at first," Patuleia remembers. "I had just been a finalist for the principalship in Revere, and I felt a little used in that case. I think they had their man from the start, and they just walked me though the process to make it look like a fair hire. And I'd heard about Lynn, that the politics were thick, that outsiders weren't always welcome. But I saw the ad, so I called a friend who had taught in Lynn, and I asked him if it was an open search. He immediately said no, there's an insider who's going to get the job. So for the moment, that settled it, I wouldn't apply. But then just by chance I picked up a newspaper and saw an article about some golf tournament that had a picture of the Lynn Schools Superintendent playing golf with one of my old teachers, a man who had helped me decide to go into administration, someone who really supported me. So I called him, and then *he* made a couple of calls and told me that they weren't really happy with the insider, he wasn't a strong runner. So I applied.

"Still, I wasn't sure it would be a good fit. So I drove down one day, just to take a look at the school, to see how it felt. I get here after school's over for the day, park the car, and I see a bunch of kids playing football, just goofing around. I call them over and we talk. I ask them about drugs in the school. They say there are some, but it's not terrible. Gangs? Also some, but not too bad. Fights? Yeah, they said, there's fights. Do the teachers care? No, they said, the teachers don't give a shit.

"I was ready to leave, but I saw a guy sitting in his car, watching the kids playing. Maybe he was waiting to pick up somebody. I walked over, and I could see he was a little drunk. I told him why I was there and I asked him about the school. He said, 'I just want you to go in there and make it safe for my daughter, because it's not safe now.' That had a real impact on me.

"So I'm a candidate, and they're interested in me. They schedule a school tour, and the guy who leads me around school is one of the old-timers, one of the guys who's not happy with idea that an outsider might come in to run his school, maybe make his job a little harder. He's showing me everything that's wrong about the school, 'This is busted,' 'That don't work,' 'These are all gone and we can't get anymore.' But I saw through it; he just wanted to discourage me.

"While we're walking through the hallways, a group of students comes through, cheerleaders coming in from practice. And I just liked them, you know? I liked the way they talked. No gossip, no nastiness. They weren't spoiled. They were polite to each other. I liked them a lot. Then on the way out of the building, when I was alone, I bumped into a group of black kids on the steps. They're asking me 'Who're you?,' kind of challenging me. So we talk, and I tell them I'm applying for the principalship, tell them what I saw in school, and I ask them, 'What do you think I should do?' They say 'Go for it, man.' And that's what I did. Mostly because of the students; I genuinely like the students. I'm from Peabody, and not the best part of Peabody. I grew up with poor kids, kids who had to work, kids who appreciated the breaks they got. So coming here, in some ways I was coming home.

"I realized when I first walked the halls at English that I'd become tired of the spoiled kids, the kids in the fancier schools.

"Now, I'm home."

Patuleia's presence is felt all over the school. One of the first substantial changes he made was to install three "monitors" in the school—well-dressed young men with discreet walkie-talkies who stroll the halls all day, herding kids into their classes, checking hall passes, establishing a presence. All three seem to be in their late twenties; two are black and one is Hispanic; all three live in Lynn and have relatives attending the school. They are the most constant reminder of Patuleia's emphasis on order, and they clearly have their effect: violence inside the school is sharply down. The monitors also remind students that they are, in fact, required to be in particular places all the time. They can get on the students' nerves, strutting through the halls between classes barking out "Get into class! Get into class!" They see part of their job as scaring kids into doing the right thing. They also have fun, and at times seem like students themselves. One monitor sees a knot of girls beside an open classroom door. He gets close and says in a bedroom whisper, "Girls, do it just for me. Go in."

Patuleia talks to students in the halls as he sweeps through. He's not a tall man, and since he took on the principalship, he's put on twenty pounds. Many students tower over him, but their deference is clear. Those who like him seem to like him a great deal—they seem to rely on him, to value his position as something of an outsider even after a year and a half in the building. He spends a lot of time walking the halls, talking to the students. When he first arrived at English High, he spent one whole day asking kids in the hall who was dealing drugs at school. "And they told me. Not at first, but eventually they told me. And I wasn't really surprised. These are good kids.

"I remember one of my teachers here—he had some duties about disciplining students—introducing himself at a parents' night as 'the guy who deals with the bad kids.' I had to talk to him later. I told him, 'There *are* no bad kids in this school. Kids with problems, yes, but no bad kids.'

"And I don't just say this. I really mean it. The best example is a kid named George. A few weeks after I got here, I was sitting in my office and I heard this explosion of sound, like the circus just came to town right outside the side door to my office. I go out there and here's this massive kid, over six feet, thick like a tree, ugly looking, mean, mad, and he's pointing his finger down at this small Hispanic kid saying 'I'm gonna kill you, motherfucker!' And he's reaching out like he's about to pick this little kid up and just smash him. I turn to the kid next to me, he's just watching the fight, I ask him 'Who's the big guy?' He says, 'That's George, Mr. Patuleia. He's bad.' Then I slide over to George, I put my hand on his forearm—I'm like a fly on an elephant—and I say into his ear, quietly, 'George. George, I need to talk to you.' He turns to me and says 'Who the fuck are you?' 'I'm the new principal, George,' real quietly, gently, 'Come on with me.' My arm still on his arm like that, I just walk him into my office.

"Well, in ten minutes, he's crying his eyes out, this big bruiser. He's just deeply, deeply sad, with real problems. We talk for a couple of hours, and I get him to agree to go into counseling. So was this a bad kid? No. This was a kid with problems. But you know, the problems were too big. Three days later, he was arrested in Boston, and that was really the end of hope for him.

"What a kid like that needs is to be taken out of his environment, taken somewhere else, where the friends who helped him down the wrong path to begin with aren't around to tempt him anymore. He needs to spend a year with really good kids,

kids with good values, and then what's inside him will start to come out. But it's hard to make that happen here. Sometimes it does happen, but with the kids with the deepest problems, it's a matter of chance as much as anything else."

Committed to the students as he may be, though, many students are at best indifferent toward Patuleia. Yes, they feel safer at English since he arrived, but they also feel more closely watched, more hemmed in. Some teachers feel the same way. One will only talk to Patuleia with the school's union representative present. Patuleia says he actually likes her, that she's just paranoid and will eventually learn to trust him.

It didn't help much that one of his first real challenges as principal ended with the ouster of a popular vice-principal, Ken Curtis. Curtis had wanted the principalship himself, but was turned down for it. In Patuleia's final job interview before he was hired, one of the Lynn school-committee members pointedly asked him how he would deal with Curtis, guessing that Curtis would be resentful. "If he does his job," Patuleia replied, "we'll have no problems at all." But some thought that Curtis *wasn't* doing his job, that he was missing too many meetings, that he was resisting Patuleia too openly, too bitterly. Patuleia wrote a letter to the superintendent, outlining problems he was having with Curtis, and the superintendent decided to transfer Curtis to one of Lynn's middle schools.

The next day, Evan had a video crew outside the building shooting a mass student walkout in protest. Patuleia had been out of the building all morning, and Evan's crew caught the confusion in his face as he got out of his car and walked towards the school. "Students were shouting at him," Evan says, "calling him names, though nothing vulgar, which actually surprised me. He went in, got a bullhorn, and came right back out."

"I get to the school," Patuleia remembers, "and it's the moment of truth. I've been at the school just a couple of months and many of the kids don't really know whether they can trust me. The teachers, too, need to see that I can deal with a problem like the problem with Curtis without losing control of the school. So all the money's riding on this. The press is there—the next day there's a picture on the cover of the *Item*—and most of the teachers are out there, but they're not telling the kids to come in, they're not working with this problem, they're just watching, smiling, seeing the show.

"At first there had been fifty or sixty students, then someone pulled the fire alarm, so by the time I got there, the whole
school was massed in front of the building, and they're calling
out Kenny Curtis's name. It was big time, high drama. I told
them I wanted to talk, but only with fifty or sixty kids, and
inside the building."

Ken Curtis's student aide, a girl named June, was one of the
leaders of the walkout. She talks with the airy accent of white,
blue-collar Lynners. "We were just totally mad at first," June
remembers. "Patuleia wanted us to come back in, into the auditorium, and we were just 'No, No, No.' But we were surprised,
really, that he *wanted* to talk, instead of saying 'Come back or
I'll kick you out of school' or something, so eventually most of
us went in. Some kids just took off for the day. They didn't
care at all, really, but most of us went into the auditorium and
we heard what Patuleia had to say. Basically, he said he respected Mr. Curtis, that Mr. Curtis was a leader, but that the
two of them wouldn't make a good team, and that Mr. Curtis
would be able to go to another school and he'd probably be
happier there anyway. Patuleia said, 'I need you to give me a
chance.' He said he would have to work for us in his own way,
that we might not always like what he did, and we didn't have
to like him personally, but that he would make a difference if
we gave him a chance. He talked to us with respect. So we did
give him a chance and it's true, he did make a difference."

"I probably told the kids more than I should have," Patuleia
says. "I probably gave them a little too much of what they
wanted, but it worked. That walkout did it—after that, they were
with me."

Patuleia points out three young teachers—two of them math
teachers—he recently hired. "These are my people," he says,
"the kind of teachers I want in every classroom." For the moment, there are not many of Patuleia's people at English High,
but he's willing to be patient. As for the others, "they're afraid
of change, and I'm making changes. Teachers get defensive.
You've got to calm them down, convince them you're not trying to fire them."

For someone who seems amused by his own occasional gruff-
ness, Patuleia is remarkably gentle in conversation with teachers—he listens quietly, always finds something to praise. But
surely many teachers can tell when good words from the boss
flow more from his management philosophy than from genu-

ine good feeling. And there are some teachers Patuleia simply dislikes. "This man," he says quietly, pointing to a teacher walking by in the hall, "is the laziest teacher I've ever met." And every time he goes into the gym, he fights the urge to brush the basketball coach aside and take over, show him how it's done. "Nothing would make me happier than finding the time to coach this basketball team. That's something I dream about."

On the inside of Patuleia's office door hangs a piece of paper with these words on it: "Good things happen to kids who follow the rules and are kind, humble, friendly, and in control. Good things happen to kids who cooperate."

Sandy doesn't think that highly of most of his teachers. Ask him who is his favorite, and he says he can't think of one. Evan's choice is easy, though: Mr. Murphy. Three girls standing with him quickly agree. "He moves around, he gets you thinking," one says. Another says, "He's alive. He hears you." Sandy and Evan are both in Bill Murphy's twelfth-grade American History class. It's an honors class, part of an honors program that about 20 percent of the students are placed into through standardized test scores and teacher recommendation. The rest of the classes at English are divided about evenly into college preparatory and "general" classes.

I waited outside one of Bill Murphy's ninth-grade general civics classes one morning as the monitors swept through. "In class. Let's move it! Come on, get in, get in." The kids in the civics class gathering behind me were as far removed from the senior honors students as they could be—these students were the youngest and, judging by test scores, the least able.

Murphy was late, and the students started coming up to me, hopeful: "You the substitute?" I'd asked the teacher who was clearing out of the room if *he* was Murphy. "No, no," he had chuckled. "Murphy looks like a salesman."

He has great hair—thick, combed back, salt and pepper— and a toothy smile. But there is an edge, a seriousness that was clearly more teacher than salesman. He is fit, and takes physical training seriously. "I believe in the Greco-Roman ideal—a sound mind and a sound body." Later, he says "The kids here need more spiritualism. I want to take them mountain climbing." He wears black slacks, a red and white striped oxford shirt and a black tie. And the Letterman touch: white hi-tops.

He swooshes in late, invites me to stay for the class, tells the students to settle down, holds up a newspaper and asks the students what's going on. He means in the city, in the country, in the world. There is chatter, giggling. "C'mon, Shanequa," he cautions a girl near the front. She keeps talking to the girl next to her. Murphy changes tack. "O.K., who was absent yesterday?" A surprisingly robust chorus of "Me's" replies. "Girls, c'mon, settle down" he says, patient but not pleased as Shanequa and her friend keep talking loudly enough to be heard across the room. Murphy jumps back to current events. Sixty-six people have been killed by mortar fire in Sarajevo while waiting for food in a central marketplace, and he holds up a *Boston Globe* with the story. Holding the newspaper high, he side-steps to a map of Europe before World War One on an oversize easel, and points to Sarajevo (which he pronounces Sara-HEY-vo). Then he puts down the newspaper and holds up a copy of *U.S. News and World Report,* with a picture of the figure–skater Nancy Kerrigan, a local Boston hero whose career has just been heightened by a celebrated whack in the knee apparently orchestrated by her rival, Tonya Harding. "I'm just sick of this," he says with a smile, leaning forward. "'Her Mental Struggle.' What mental struggle? Give me a break."

I sit in back of the class. To my right are two beefy, unwashed white kids, eyeing each other with ambitious cynicism, making small, bitter jokes and odd noises. In front of me, a pale, freckled girl with red hair and a narrow chin sucks on a lollipop, looking around but seeming not to see anything. Up in front of my row of desks a morose black girl sits with her head on her arm. Over toward the right, Shanequa and her friend are still animated, but not loud. Written on the little gray writing desk bolted to my chair: "Fuck Corporate Rock," "Just Say No to Corporate Rock," "Pathetic!," "Everyone is Fucking Pathetic," and the names of rock groups. "The Mighty Boss Tones." "Black Flag." Others.

Murphy doesn't seem to be getting much response, but his energy is admirable. He bounces around, smiles hard, leans forward and tries to strike a spark. He's back on Sara-HEY-vo, trying to explain the issue of credibility that the United States and the U.N face today, having repeatedly threatened the Serbian soldiers and militia killing Bosnian civilians but without following through. He uses the example of two girls who were late for class the other day. He told them they'd have to stay late and offer a pretty persuasive excuse. They didn't; they just left at the end of the period. "Now, if I don't do anything, if I just let this go after I said they had to see me, I lose credibility." A large girl in a chair near mine says with disgust, just loud enough for Murphy to hear, "Like you never late."

One boy, all the way on the other side of the room, near the door, has his chair-with-desk turned precisely sideways, and sits looking into the wall three feet in front of him. Murphy turns back to *U.S. News* and Nancy Kerrigan. "Why does she get the whole front page? Why is she news?" No one answers. "You know a policeman was shot yesterday in Boston." A couple of kids say "Um hmm"; a bit of energy stirs. "A kid, nineteen years old, he shot a cop. He was driving the wrong way down a one-way street, the cop stopped him, and he shot the cop." The class is listening carefully. Murphy's energy rises, too: yet higher. He steps back to a blackboard—really it's green, with large yellow splotches that won't hold chalk. He's filled it earlier in the day with briefs of news stories from the papers and magazines—and he points to a terse summary of the policeman's killing. He brightens. "Now, if you ever are arrested—and I hope none of you are ever arrested—keep your mouth shut!" A couple of heads pop up, but seeing Murphy there, they lose their focus quickly enough; they seem to have heard this before, but they are not immune to a moment's excitement when a teacher breaks out of his role and becomes a jailhouse lawyer. "Keep your mouth shut! This kid, do you know what he said to the cop who arrested him? 'I wish I had another bullet for you.'" A small murmur near Shanequa. "This will be used against him—he should have kept his mouth shut. And whatever you do, don't use foul language. Cops hate that. Especially if you're female." Still, Murphy's appeal to their darker sides is merely tolerated; he's done this kind of thing before, and the students congratulate themselves with small groans of discontent for how well they've withheld their interest against all odds.

Back again to Nancy Kerrigan and *U.S. News*: "Why is she on the cover, week after week, magazine after magazine? Do we really need to know more about her? Or should we know more about that cop who was shot? Should his picture be on

the cover? Or the kid who shot him? Don't we need to understand more about this kid than about Nancy Kerrigan?"

Murphy mentions a book he's just read about Michael Jordan. "You know it's Black History Month, and this is a great
book. I got it right here at the library." The first serious reply
of the class comes as a surprise: "Michael Jackson's gonna play
baseball." It's Shanequa. Murphy smiles, jumps a tiny jump in
the air, and repeats, "Michael Jackson's gonna play baseball."
He pauses for a minute, his smile droops for a split second,
but returns as he offers an amiable retraction. "No, no. Michael
Jordan's gonna play baseball." Shanequa is pleased along with
Murphy, happy to get it right, "Michael Jordan. Michael Jordan," she says. Murphy fills in the details: Michael Jordan
signed with a baseball team to train with them in the preseason.
Murphy talks about how hard it is on the body to play two
professional sports, and mentions a ballplayer none of the students have ever heard of. Someone volunteers Bo Jackson's
name, and the first swirl of discussion for the day picks up.
Murphy cautions them all to train carefully, to go slow and
steady with athletics. He points to a girl in the class whom he's
seen in the school's weight–training room, congratulating her
on doing it well, and puffs himself up a bit as he talks about
his own weight lifting.

Then he moves into the official business of the day's civics
lesson: the presidency. A couple of students open their big
hard-cover texts. Murphy reminds them that in their last class
meeting they hadn't been thrilled with the idea that the president had to be born in the United States—a few of the students
are themselves immigrants, and about half are the children of
families from the Dominican Republic, Haiti, or Central
America. Today they begin with the question of the minimum
age requirement for the president, and soon they discuss
Ronald Reagan's age, and his frequent naps. About half the
students seem to be paying attention, and two or three answer
questions intermittently. Murphy bounces around the room,
pointing to covers of *Time* and *Newsweek* hanging on the walls—
here's Reagan, here's Carter. He mentions Geraldine Ferraro,
and a few students seem genuinely surprised that a woman
had made it onto the ticket. Then he reaches back to his favorite topic, the foolishness of magazines: when Ferraro's

runningmate first made news, the magazines wrote again and
again about his haircut, at the expense of his ideas. He points
to a *Time* magazine cover of Mondale and his prominent bad
haircut. "But what about Jesse Jackson?" he asks. Half the students in the class are black, and a few show real interest. Murphy
says that Jackson's speech to the 1988 Democratic National
Convention was amazing, historic. Someone asks why he got
to give a speech—he lost the election, right? Murphy leaps toward the question, a real question, an intelligent question, to
explain how the party nominating conventions work, how the
nomination is won, how power is brokered.

But, he says, lots of people said we weren't ready for a black
president, that if Jackson were elected, he'd be shot, so it would
be best not to vote for him at all. The two heavyset white boys
next to me make guns with their fingers and shoot. One girl,
unheard from so far, says, "They won't vote for him because
he's black. That's all." Murphy talks about stereotypes generally, then about Irish stereotypes in particular, and conjures
the picture of John F. Kennedy taking calls from the Pope on
domestic policy. "Because we're everywhere, you know, look
at all the Murphys and O'Neills in the phone book. We're taking over, and look out, because you know those Irish," and he
tips an imaginary glass. "But these are just stereotypes. Stereotypes! They're not true.

"But Clinton, as I told you, is vulnerable. He's made en-
emies—in the military, gays, with health care. Don't be surprised, as I've said, if he winds up assassinated. Shot." The
boys next to me make shooting sounds again, and one of them
whispers, "Blow his fucking head off." They chuckle. "But where
does violence get us?" Murphy asks, as sincere as anyone can
be asking this kind of question. He scans the room, wanting
every kid there to take his caution seriously, to heed him for
their own sakes. "Ooooo," says Shanequa, ready to offer an
observation about violence, "there was a fight today. Five girls,
over a boy." Everyone's interested, a couple of different kids
throw out stray facts—what time, who the girls were, who the
boy was. The boy was David, the golf-club victim. Apparently,
he's popular.

David's never had Mr. Murphy, but he's heard of him. "He's
the funny one," his friend Grady says, "with that hair." David

nods; yes, he knows him, but David doesn't seem to have much of an opinion of him. He's better in math and science. He's doing well in algebra—earning an A—though he's a year behind because of his grades in ninth grade. "Straight flags," he says— straight F's. Grady is more interested in Murphy, though he hasn't had him for a class either. But English and social studies are his favorite subjects, and he is one of the few black students at Lynn English who wants to talk about race. Most others seem ashamed of the whole question, as though to talk about race is to talk about some deficiency of theirs. Grady is not ashamed. He talks with a hint of anger, but calmly. When I ask, he says he likes English High, that it's a good school even though it gets a bad rap. But he doesn't really like the teachers. I realize that most students, when I ask about English High generally, think I'm talking about the students. If it's a bad school, they must be bad students. If it's good, they're good. So Grady defends the school, says it's better than people in other towns think it is. But he'd never send his own kids to English, he says, because of the teachers, especially the history teachers. "I would want my kids to learn about the world, you know? More than the books, more than the little bit of knowledge the teachers put in a box and take it over to you and say here, here it is, take it if you want it. We always talk about slavery, always. Like that's it, nothing more, nothing black people ever did, nothing happening anywhere else. I'm tired of it. Why don't they teach us about when we had gold and we were kings and queens?"

Grady's grades are good, but his SAT scores are low. He has Jane Turner, one of the two black teachers in the school, for English this term. "She helps me more than any white teacher ever helped me. I told three different teachers where I want to go to college—Villanova, University of Texas—and they're like, 'You want to go there? Think again.' She's working for me, though, she's helping me write my essays, saying yes, I can do it, I can go for it." Grady, like more than half the black male students I meet at English, wants to be a professional athlete— a basketball player. His second career choice, and it is a second choice just as common among the black English High students, is to own his own business. He scorns the racial stereotypes around him. "You come into school with a new pair of sneakers two days in a row, wear a gold chain, get a new jacket, everybody says, 'Oh, you're dealing drugs.' Why can't we spend our money any way we want? My parents work, they make money. Why can't a black man buy a new goddamn jacket without being a criminal?" Grady seems aware that his dream of playing professional ball is tainted by those stereotypes, but he loves to play. He has carefully inspected his hopes, and chosen to keep them.

Grady has white friends at school, but he is bitter that they never invite him to their homes. "They don't want us in their house. Maybe we'll steal something. I don't know. I just don't know." He shakes his head, sadly. David looks at his friend and adds, "That's how it's always going to be. It's never going to change."

The schoolday ends at two-thirty every day. Half an hour later, three young women and one boy wait for the clock to run out on their after-school detention. They have five more minutes to wait. The boy looks small and frail; next to the others, three self-possessed seniors, he seems like the younger brother, or the son. He sits apart, his red hair and freckled face pointing straight down at a blank desk. Angie is among the three others. She missed her English class three times last week. She won't say why—any number of excuses would probably suffice—so she's here in detention. The two others flirt with Mark Anderson, the monitor who wound up with detention duty today. "It's time, Mark," one of them says. "Don't you want to let us go, show us how much you like us?" Angie, too, is not above adding to Mark's obvious discomfort, though all she says is "please."

Angie is going to college next term, which makes her an English High success story. She's applied to Northeastern and to Boston University, though if she's not offered hefty scholarships she'll probably wind up at the local public college, Salem State. On a warm day, you could walk from English High to Salem State in about an hour, though no one does; some of the worst parts of Lynn lie between the two schools, areas designed to have the feel of real back country, with fingers of a state park reaching out between streets of old, large homes. Today the homes are all either low-rent rooming houses or abandoned. The strips of parkland are desolate and dangerous, zones of darkness set down among the very worst streets in the city of Lynn. Angie lives far from those troubled streets, on Chatham Street, a busy road closer to the school. "It's nice; nicer, at least, than some other parts of Lynn." She's planning on being a doctor.

Angie's feelings about English High don't run very deep. "It's not a great school, but it's been good enough for me. I've learned what I've had to learn. No one's gotten in my way, but I can't point to anyone and say this teacher showed me something I needed to see."

She doesn't like the emphasis on sports. "Too many of these boys follow the bouncing ball when they should be thinking about other things. I call them boys. They are boys, the boys I'm talking about. I can't say there are many young men here, really, though there are a few. But it's too easy to get along here, to be popular and to lead the teachers along, having them think you're O.K., you've got a good name, because you play basketball or football.

"Here at this school, if you fight, the teachers and the principal, they put you on a little list, this is a bad kid, and they try to let you know, we're watching you. If you do honors classes, they put you on another list, we know you're smart, we're gonna help you go to college. If you're not serious about your classes but you're on a team, you go to practice, they put you on the list that says you may not be a smart kid, but maybe you can be trusted.

"But I don't like that. There's no big fights between the black students and the white students, but look at the teams. Who's on the teams from the white kids? Kids with good grades, and they play ball. Who's on the teams from the black kids? Kids who get bad grades. Playing on a team isn't just for competition or whatnot for those black kids, it's to prove something to the teachers, to prove they can go along with the program, you understand? Prove they can be part of something good. But they make it too easy here for these boys to give up thinking I can go to college, I can be an honors student, I can be better at my classes. They say, well, you can play ball, you can show up and take orders, then that's enough, we know you're a good kid, you've done enough. I don't like that. For the girls there's the cheerleading, but that's not the same. The girls don't say,

'Well I'm a cheerleader, that's enough for my life's dream.' But I know too many boys who say, 'Well, I'm gonna play basketball, that's enough, that's a great thing.'

"You go to the gym, look over at the principal, see how he looks when some black kid puts the basketball in the hoop. You know he's as happy with you as he's ever gonna be. It's a high prize, it says you did enough with that ball playing, you earned your keep here at English, so don't worry.

"Let me tell you, my family is a good family, my parents work and they work good jobs and my mother's been to college and I'm going to college, too. But I worry all the time. I come to school in the morning, I worry: Will I walk out at the end of the day and know enough to take my tests and get some scholarship money to buy my books? Will I learn enough to get advanced credit so I'll graduate from college maybe a little early? Every damn day I come in here I worry. You know what else I worry about? I worry about those boys I see jumping for the hoop, I worry if they can read a goddamn book. I wouldn't walk out in public with half the boys I see here in school. I will not be seen with ignorant boys."

Angie's anger builds as she talks. Then she stops, and then she starts talking again, in a different key. "I feel good about myself. I'm walking out of this school with a good diploma. The school was dangerous when I first got here, three years ago. There was no principal, really. Two new ones came and left in one year. There were fights every day in the cafeteria. Sometimes black and white, sometimes Spanish and black. It was hard. I hated it. I walked home and I looked over my shoulder. If I was walking home and someone ran past me, I knew someone was chasing him, he'd come past me too, I could count, one, two, three, there he is, number two runs right past me, then number three, number four. Everybody wants to be close to the fight, everybody wants to see it.

"I saw one guy kicked in the head when I was walking home last year. This boy, he ran past me but two others were right behind him reaching out and they got him, they grabbed the back of his shirt and you could see him for a minute running through the shirt, from the back to the front of it, stretching it out, but they got him and one kid punched him in the back of the head. He fell down, the other kid just stopped. He was running, but he just stopped real fast and popped him right across the nose with his boot. Then they just left him. They weren't even angry. And the kid got up, he was full of blood, but he got up and took off his shirt and held it to his face and he just walked away.

"But it's been better this year. The school feels more together. But they're not changing the problems, I think. They're not reaching the kids who were fighting and making them learn. They're making them not fight. That's different.

"But if you ask me, do I feel safe? Yes, I feel safe enough. I do my business here, I stay away from the people who want to have problems, I don't get bothered. Usually, I'm just not thinking about violence at school. It's not in front of me, it's not in my way. Today, I'm not thinking about it."

Today, on the third floor, one teacher at English High *is* thinking about violence. She is a veteran teacher, fifteen years in the building, and right now she's a bit shaky. She leaves a note for the principal, and he comes to her classroom door not long after, at about ten o'clock, while she's teaching. She tells her students to work quietly at their seats and excuses herself. She pulls Patuleia close to her and starts talking, with real fear in her voice. Yesterday, a student had cursed her in class. "He ridiculed me. Ridiculed! In front of the whole class. I took him down to the vice-principal's office and insisted he be suspended. The vice-principal said yes, O.K., he'd take care of it, I should leave the kid there. So I did. But the rest of the day, there he was in school, and every time I walked by him in the hallway, he was talking to his friends in Spanish, laughing at me. I shouldn't have to take that. I should not. Absolutely not."

Patuleia says she's right. He'll look into it. Come to my office later, he says. He touches her on the arm, to reassure her. He says, "You're one of the people I count on."

He heads down to the office. The office is actually a large reception room with a waist-high counter running its width, separating students and visitors from the busy collection of secretaries on its other side. Behind the secretaries, a short corridor opens onto a warren of offices, two for the vice-principals, one for the photocopy machine, one filled with outdated office equipment, and an administrators' bathroom. The vice-principal Patuleia needs to see is in. He sits behind his desk, looking confused as a student stands in his office and cries. The student seems totally lost in grief. Ingrid Moreno, one of the school's guidance counselors, is in the vice-principal's small office, too. She comforts the student as the vice-principal looks on. Patuleia walks in, concerned. "Are you all right?" he asks the student. She tries to regain her composure, but can't. "I've got it, I'm with her," Moreno says, and she guides her toward a back door, then across the main hallway, and over to her own office.

Patuleia is left with the man he came to see. The walls of the vice-principal's office are covered with lists of students—one list is the day's absentees; another, recent graduates; a third, former students barred from entering the building. And, oddly, a large picture of Hubert Humphrey.

Patuleia asks him about the student accused of harassing the English teacher. "Yes, he's suspended. He's out," says the vice-principal, a fastidious man wearing dated black-framed glasses. He stops and thinks for a moment. "What's his name? He's got that hyphenated name." His name is Estaban Hernandez. The vice-principal looks up his record and says, "This may not be a kid we want to go easy on." A few months ago, he was found carrying a knife in school. Then, taking Patuleia by surprise, the vice-principal asks, "Didn't we take a gun off him once?"

He continues: "Does he speak English?" Then, "Wasn't he involved with that kidnapping?"

He was. Two months earlier, the *Lynn Item* ran a front-page story headlined "Lynner Escapes Violent Kidnap":

A Holland Avenue man was kidnapped and beaten Sunday afternoon by three men looking for the tenant who rented his garage.

Charged with kidnapping, armed assault with intent to rob and assault and battery with a dangerous weapon, a shod foot, were Carlos Contreras, 21, 83 Walnut Street, Kilvio Fernandez, 21, 100 Franklin Street, and Estaban Hernandez, 17, Lloyd Street, all of Lynn.

As Mary Luttgens watched from a window, a car pulled up in front of her home. Before her horrified eyes three men got out and one put a handgun in the trunk of the car.

Mrs. Luttgens jotted down the license number of the car as the men approached her home. At the door, they asked for her husband. They told James Luttgens they wanted to speak to the man he rented his garage to and Luttgens said he would go with them to help them find him.

Luttgens said they drove around for a short time, looking for his tenant without success, and one of the men suggested they go to Barry Park and play basketball.

When they got out of the car, however, the trio surrounded Luttgens, beating and kicking him, demanding that he tell them where his tenant was.

Luttgens said he didn't know where the tenant was, but the men continued to hit him. They finally forced him back into the car and drove to the Henry Avenue Playground, where the interrogation scene was repeated.

At one point in the car, one of the men suggested getting his Glock— a name for a particular make of handgun—from the car trunk and shooting Luttgens.

Patuleia gingerly reminds the vice-principal of his policy for suspending students. If the student has made any kind of threat to a teacher, he's suspended immediately, personally escorted to the front door by the vice-principal. A mistake was made with this kid. He shouldn't have been allowed to remain in school once the teacher had brought him to the vice-principal. He shouldn't have been in hallways later that same day, frightening his teacher.

In the afternoon, the teacher tells several people about Estaban, and every time she tells the story she mentions his friends in hallways: "They were talking in Spanish, laughing at me." She doesn't speak Spanish, and when she began teaching at Lynn English, there wasn't much call for bilingual teachers. Today, about one third of all English High students come from Spanish speaking homes. Some speak English fluently—many were born in Lynn, though most of their parents were born in the Dominican Republic or Central America—some don't speak English at all, and most are somewhere in between.

Ingrid Moreno is officially a bilingual guidance counselor, though in fact she is fluent in Spanish, French, Italian, and German, as well as English. In the hall, she can be heard calling to Dominican students in Spanish, and Haitian students in French.

"I have two jobs at this school," she says, "to change the behavior of the students, and to change the behavior of the teachers. Almost every teacher in this school has no comfort outside of English, outside of their own lives. They see a kid who speaks Spanish and is learning English, who works after school and takes care of his parents and his brothers and sisters and maybe his child, and they see this student as a student with a problem, a deficiency."

An outsider can't help wondering: If Estaban's English teacher spoke Spanish, wouldn't she be less frightened of him? But there are other questions, too. On a street in Lynn where the families speak Spanish—and there are many such streets in Lynn—when they read in the paper about how Estaban Hernandez and Carlos Contreras and Kilvio Fernandez beat a man and threatened to kill him with a gun, are those families any less afraid?

Estaban Hernandez represents an important contradiction that lies near the heart of Lynn English High School's prospects. More than most, he needs Lynn English to help him change, but his presence in the school is uncomfortable, and perhaps even dangerous, for other students and teachers. Take the view of Estaban's parent, and you realize that the school has not given him enough. It is place where teachers and administrators think of his name as odd ("He has that hyphenated name," the vice-principal said), and clearly fear him ("Didn't we take a gun off him once?" No, Estaban has never been found with a gun.) But take the view of the parent of any one of Estaban's classmates, and you see value in Patuleia's final dispensation: Estaban is out, for good. He won't be returning to Lynn English High.

His former English teacher feels safer, more comfortable in the hallways. Estaban will be directed to alternative programs, most likely to equivalency-degree study courses. The school will be an easier place to teach and learn without Estaban around.

But what will Estaban learn? And what will the others—students and teachers—have learned about Estaban? Bill Murphy's words about the 19-year-old boy who killed a Boston policeman seem important: Don't we need to know more about this kid?

Chapter Two

Lessons

A *Boston Globe* article brings some unwanted attention to the public schools of Lynn on a cold February morning. In the metro section, a headline announces "Lynn Youth Shot Dead; 2nd Wounded." Two students at Lynn Classical High School, English High's crosstown rival, were shot the day before—Valentine's Day—in front of a pizza place near school. One died, the other was paralyzed. The killer escaped.

At English the next morning, Patuleia speaks briefly to students over the school's closed-circuit television system, and calls for a moment of silence and reflection. At lunch, most English students go about business as usual—eating, flirting, standing in line. But many talk about the shooting.

There is a degree of racial self-segregation in the cafeteria, but only a small degree. Three tables are wholly separate: a table of Asian males, most of them recent immigrants; a table of Russian immigrants, most of them male; and a table of white male athletes. Twenty other tables are a mix of colors, accents, shapes and sizes.

One group of young women sits together and loudly fills out computer dating forms. "Am I shy?" asks one of them. She answers her own question: "No. How do I spend most Saturday nights? I hate to say it, but it's true. Dateless!" A friend also checks the "dateless" box on her own form, and they share some sympathetic laughter. These young women are a diverse group—one is black, one is Asian, and two are Hispanic, but their obvious concern for each other overwhelms their ethnic differences. One plans to be a doctor, a pediatrician; she sits quietly, volunteering little, but speaks at length when asked a serious question. Another is loud, joking about her computer dating form with everyone who passes by the table; she plans to become a lawyer. A third is less self-assured than the others, but she too is decisive about her future: she plans to be an engineer. The last of the group, perhaps daunted by her friends' ambitions, says she is between career plans.

They talk about the shooting. They sympathize with the victims: the horror and the waste are obvious to them. But each reveals a hardness as she talks. These are not young women of privilege. They are from poor families, and in their own eyes they stand apart from the young people they know who deal drugs and do crimes not because of money or status but because of character. The aspiring physician offers an illustration of bad character: "Remember that Spanish boy who got shot by Mackie and that other guy on Chestnut Street in August? I was standing with him five minutes before. I liked him, but he knew he was in trouble. It was his trouble, he made it for himself. It wasn't no accident." She won't elaborate, but like the others, she blames the boy who died outside of Classical High for living a bad life. He was sixteen, but didn't live at home. She says she knows a boy fifteen who doesn't live at home either. "His parents hate him, because of how he acts. He goes with his mother, stays until she throws him out because he steals her things or fights with her, then he goes to his father and then the same thing happens, so he goes and stays maybe at a friend's house till his friend throws him out and by then maybe his mother or his father forgets what a scumbag he is and they let him back in, so it starts all over again, but you couldn't say he lives in one place."

Her friend who plans to be an engineer hears this and says that they all need to leave Lynn as soon as they can—they should all go to college far away from here. "I won't stay in this area for college," she says, "And I certainly won't be back in Lynn. Not because it's dangerous; I really don't think it is dangerous. Kids get shot anywhere. There's nothing so hard about this town. It could have been somewhere else, those boys getting shot like that." She was born in the Dominican Republic, but she's been in the U.S. for twelve years. "I'm in a lot of honors classes, but I'm the only Hispanic in most of them. There's usually me, and there's one black girl, and then everybody else is white." Why don't more Hispanic students do well at English High? "It's their upbringing."

She means a couple of different things by this. First, she realizes that they don't have the kind of support for their studies that they would have if their parents spoke English well and knew how the American education system works. "Like my parents," she says, with irritation. "My parents want me to go to college but they don't even know what a term paper is." More Spanish-speaking faculty would make a great difference, "to help these students understand that they are supposed to be good at these things they have to do at school." But there's more. By "upbringing" she also means values. She sees the large block of students at English High who leave school without much hope—many of them are Dominican, like her, or black, like the 16-year-old boy at Classical who died at lunch yesterday. What can the school do to reach them? She hardens with this question. "Nothing. Nothing. If they look back at what they can do here and they still turn away, do the drugs and do the crimes, there's nothing anybody can do. If they don't have a hunger for it, nobody will convince them to do the right thing. They don't think they have a problem. That's it. They choose what they are. That's the problem."

Lunch ends, and the lunch crowd scatters. The lawyer-to-be heads to the third floor, to Mr. Murphy's classroom. She doesn't go in, but she calls a tall young woman over to her in the doorway. "Marsha! I'm here to get my dollar! Give it up, now." Marsha gets up from her seat and starts chatting with her friend in the doorway, though she doesn't hand over any money. As they talk, Murphy takes attendance. Someone in the class calls out, "Mr. Murphy, I heard what happened to you. Tonya Harding kicked you in the knee." Everyone laughs.

This is a twelfth-grade Multicultural History class, an elective. As Murphy calls out a name on the roll, Marsha turns in the doorway, extends her arm and points dramatically at Murphy. "She's cutting," Marsha says, "and she's gonna fight after school!" Murphy weighs the significance of this information, then proceeds on to call the rest of the roll. Two boys from Russia sit along the back wall. "Where's Serge?" Murphy asks, as he calls out the last name on his roster. "He got dismissed," says Marsha, "for good." This has an impact on

Murphy, but soon enough he's into his lesson, holding up a *Boston Globe*. "Look at this," he says, "the Russians are mothballing three big ships because they're too expensive to keep at sea. You don't remember this, but during the Reagan administration, we spent billions and billions and billions of dollars to match the Soviets ship for ship, and to do more—to frighten them with the size of our fleet." He calls out the names of different ships and the millions of dollars each cost to build and upkeep. "This was our lifeblood back then, our nation's most important mission, at least according to Mr. Reagan. But now the Russians are stepping back. No more billions and billions on the warships. Maybe they'll build some new schools."

He reads out the names of the Russian ships, stumbles on the last, and strides over towards the Russian students in the back of the room. "How do you say this?" "Novisikorsk," says one of the Russians. "Novisikorsk," says Murphy, calm for a moment before bursting into his next round of exposition: "*The U.S.S. Vincennes* has 5,000 men on board! Can you believe that? It's really a floating airport, an amazing thing. But you and I are paying for it." Marsha asks, "Is that where our money goes?" Murphy likes this question. "You bet. And then, look at this woman in the paper: 'Roxbury Mother Scalds Four-Year-Old Son.' This woman had had problems before, so she was being supervised by a social worker, but through a private agency contracted by the state. Cheaper that way, save some tax dollars. But they did a rotten job; the boy was scalded on his arm clear to the bone. We don't have the money to do better. No money for alternative schools. No money for extra books in the schools, for extra programs after school, for people out there to work with the kids. No money. But we've got 5,400 men out at sea on the *Vincennes*.

"So here are the Russians mothballing some ships, to save some of that money. They're making some priorities clear. They know it has to be done. We don't seem to know that yet."

Murphy points to another front-page story in the *Globe*, about Bosnia. A scruffy boy in an Army fatigue jacket quickly raises his hand and calls out, "Why is the U.S. getting involved? Why don't we let them fight their own war?" "The answer," Murphy says, "is markets, which means money. Let me explain. Take a look at the *Globe*: 'U.S., Japan Talks Fail; Interest Rates Rise.'

Our markets are connected, so when trade seems to be in danger, interest rates here go up, and that has practical effects. Rates go up, you don't buy that new car or that new house. How many jobs in the U.S. come from auto sales? A lot. How many come from home sales? Even more. Even me—I had a great job that was housing related, selling washers and driers and refrigerators at Sears to add to my teaching income. I had that job for almost ten years, until `91, when everybody in Massachusetts stopped buying houses. So it's that direct-trade talks in Japan crap out, Mr. Murphy or some other poor slob loses a couple hundred bucks a week. Europe falls apart—and this Bosnia thing could be the first step in something much bigger—the same thing happens, but worse.

"Now, how do we know some joker with a mustache and grenade thrower in Sara-HEY-vo can make trouble for the great nations of Europe? You know the answer. World War One. World War One. Archduke Ferdinand—you remember Archduke Ferdinand—assassinated in Sara-HEY-vo. That was the beginning of the first war, which led, eventually, to the Second World War, and the concentration camps. And that's the other reason—though maybe it's really still part of the first reason—that some people say we shouldn't let them fight their own wars, because they kill innocent people, sometimes by the thousands, by the millions. If that's happening, if there are atrocities—key word, atrocities—then maybe we should step in and say this is wrong, we won't let you kill these innocent people, it's just too horrible to sit back and watch."

A student near the window has been listening carefully, but is not convinced. "Markets, huh?" "Yes, yes," Murphy says sharply, bouncing over to the window. "Markets. Look at what we're doing now in Vietnam. We've just dropped the economic sanctions that began with our war there. Just now. But why? Markets. American companies are aching to get in there and trade. They want that, and the government responds. We dragged through that war year after year after year, but when there's trade to be had, money to be made, hey, let bygones be bygones, because other nations are moving their companies in and making real dollars. So Vietnam's O.K. Now, look across the water in Florida, you see Cuba—we've still got trade sanctions against Cuba, they're a bunch of communists, we say, but

come on, are they any worse than Vietnam? The real difference? The real difference between Cuba and Vietnam? Money
to be made in the markets of Vietnam. Cuba, no. Not yet. So
the sanctions stay, and we talk about how rotten Castro is—his
daughter just fled to the U.S., says the old man is a dictator,
maybe Castro had something to do with killing JFK, he keeps
political prisoners. All this might be true, but if there was trade
money to be made, you'd see how quickly we would grant for-
giveness."

Murphy takes a breath and surveys the class—they're quiet,
maybe bored. He picks up his copy of *U.S. News and World
Report,* with a cover story about the film *Shindler's List.* "Did
anyone see this film?" Out of twenty-five students, one student
half-raises his hand. "This," he says to the student in the fatigue jacket who had asked why we don't let the former Yugo-
slavia fight its own wars, "this is part of the reason we say we
have to do something. After the Second World War, when we
saw the camps and the pits and the men and women and children half-dead in the prisons, the League of Nations, which
later became the United Nations, said no, no, we won't let this
happen again."

He circles back to the article on Japanese trade. Holding it
up, he says. "Do you remember when President Bush threw up
on the Japanese Prime Minister a couple of years ago?" To most
of the students, this is a surprise, but an amusing surprise.
"Oh yes, yes he did. Why was he there? Trade talks. The big
man, the president goes there to make a deal, to grease the
skids to keep the markets flowing, but maybe he had some bad
sushi or something, and—" He steps forward dramatically, toward an older student, a black woman who had left English
High eight years earlier when she had a baby, and is back now
to finish her studies. She sits in the front row, follows the lesson closely. But when Murphy mimes throwing up in her lap,
she grabs her neighbor's arm and shrieks, "He threw up on
me!" They dissolve into laughter, almost falling out of their
chairs.

Murphy laughs, too. As the class regains its calm, he decides to shift gears. He walks to his desk and picks up a copy of
the day's issue of the *Lynn Item.* The headline blares "Shocker
at Classical," and under it, "Teen Shot Dead At Pizzeria Near

School." "What do you think of this," he asks, and the class stirs, agitated, engaged. "Do you think they'll catch this person?" "Yeah," say a few. "Nope," says the mother in the front row. A student near the front says, "Everybody knows who it is, they just too afraid to turn them in. When they offer some money, they'll give him up." Murphy takes a moment to absorb that, perhaps thinking about his lesson on war and markets.

"How does this affect the reputation of the Lynn schools?" Murphy asks, without getting much of a response. He keeps on: "You're a mother," he says to the woman in front. "Shouldn't we protect the kids when this kind of thing happens, shouldn't we find something to do?" She nods her head forcefully, says "Yes, uh-huh." "Maybe lock the doors at lunchtime," Murphy suggests, but he's just baiting the class. The boy in the fatigue jacket bites: "Why punish everyone for the acts of one person? Anyway, this guy was looking for those two kids, it's not like they did anything that keeping them in at lunch would have prevented. The shooter would have got them after school instead, if the doors were locked. No big difference, really. That'd just be a short-term solution to a long-term problem." Murphy beams; he recognizes this last remark—he's said the same thing to his students, and he's happy to see that it penetrated, at least in this student's case. The boy continues, "This could have happened anywhere."

"Why," asks Murphy, "don't we ever pick up the paper and see a story, 'Thousands Happy At Lynn High Schools,' why don't we hear about what we do well? Look at us, white people, black people, Spanish, Russian, Dominican, Haitian, we're together and we're doing fine here, we're not killing each other, we're accomplishing something big here. Why don't we read about that?"

His question hangs in the air. The class is focused on Murphy—they've taken his words seriously. He's quiet for a moment, and then he reads some of the details of the shooting. The shooter came in to the pizzeria, walked out with two young men who'd been eating there, put a pistol to the head of one, shot, he fell; pointed at the other, shot, he turned and ran, fired again, and the second victim fell. Murphy stretches out his arms as though he's gathering everyone in, and says, "It's amazing, when you think about it, what the brain does, the thoughts, feelings, the depth of experience in that small part of the body, the way everything connects there, and remains there, every thought, every impulse, every feeling." He brings his right hand to his head, holding a small piece of yellow chalk up against his temple, and says, "amazing what a bullet can do, a small thing, into the brain."

Murphy's next class is Honors American History, the one Evan and Sandy both attend. Evan comes in early, talks about the news show he put out that morning at school. They'd wanted to run a report of the shooting and offer some student reactions; Patuleia said no. Patuleia came on himself, after the student news show, said a few words about the shooting and then asked for a moment of silence. "Did he say to pray?" Murphy asks. "I heard he asked for a prayer." Evan doesn't think so.

Murphy's bulletin board lists some of the days news:

1) In the hills of Bosnia, Serbs stay defiant. U.S. radar-tracking units being called in. U.N. commander on the ground will make decision to call in air strikes. More U.S. aircraft arrive (F15's).
2) Prison inmate to allow a video of his execution in the gas chamber.
3) Roxbury: 4-year-old boy's hands burned to the bone by 26-year-old mother.
4) Dominican groups get tight hold of drug trade in New England towns.

Sandy comes in and says "Shh! Shh!" to the room. The before-class chatter goes on anyway. He sits in the last row and says to Marsha—Marsha's in both of Murphy's back-to-back classes—"Hey, when you gonna call me?" She ignores him, though he keeps asking, even after the lesson's begun. Finally, Marsha turns to Sandy and says sharply, "Number One, I don't have your number. Number Two, I gotta work. Number Three, why would I want to call you?"

Murphy's lesson in this class is substantial. He begins with news about Bosnia, and cuts quickly to their official topic—the causes of World War One. He tolerates less noise and crosstalk in this class than in the others. Several times, he raises his voice: "Excuse Me!" he'll say, "will you please be quiet?" In about forty minutes, he covers a lot of ground—the Zimmerman Document, connections to the Mexican American War, German culture at the turn of the century—and he locates every important city and nation on one of the three maps pulled down from concealed rollers along the front of the room. He tries to impress upon the students how distant Europe seemed to Americans early in the century—the vast separateness between the European and American continents in days of low-tech print media and travel by ship. He seems to be making it all clear—there's virtually no talk in the room, most of the students keep their eyes on Murphy, and many take notes. Murphy's working hard, keeping a steady flow of information coming, to keep the connections between all the pieces—the Archduke, the Kaiser, the Ambassador—crystal clear. He seems to be succeeding. He mentions the birth of the Selective Service Act and flickers of draft resistance as the war began, and then a girl in the back asks, "So why did we go in, if we had to draft people into the army? They didn't want to go, and didn't you say Hitler didn't even want us there anyway? So why'd we go in?"

Hitler. Wrong war. But Murphy tries to salvage the meaning of what he's been saying, and he's glad that this student is at least making some connections between different points he's mentioned. He takes a little time to talk about American resistance to entering World War Two, and how that related to the First World War. But he likes talking about the Second World War, and he goes on for a few minutes, explaining why Hitler feared U.S. entry into the war. "Hitler had just invaded Russia, and that was his first big mistake. Everything went wrong. The Germans took a lot of ground early on, but they found that when they tried to hook up their railroad system to the Russians'—they wanted to ship their arms and food and other supplies out to their army as it advanced through Russia—the size of the tracks was different. There was a standard European gauge, but the Russian train system had been built by an American Irishman, and he built the track to the American standards. So everything began taking longer than they'd expected in Russia, and the troops had only been provisioned with summer uniforms. They figured their victory would be quick, and if not, they'd have the trains haul out winter gear, but it was going slow, the trains didn't mesh, and then Mussolini, Hitler's ally in Italy, had the bright idea of invading Greece. Yep. It was those damned Italians! They really screwed things up." He gestures extravagantly over toward a young woman in the class. "You know I'm Italian, Mr. Murphy," she says with a smile, "why do you want to give me a hard time?" He says, "Who's Greek here?" Another woman in the corner raises her hand, but shyly. He won't pick on her. "Hurray for the Greeks!" he shouts. "The Germans had to rush south to help the Italians, who had bitten off more than they could chew, and that drew troops away from the Russian Front, so the last thing in the world they wanted was the U.S. to enter the war just then. But it happened anyway. But I'm getting ahead of myself," he says. "Back to World War One."

He talks about the Americans who joined the French Army before the U.S. entered the war. "They really believed in stopping the Germans and the Turks and Austro-Hungarians. They felt that something real was at stake here, that this war had all the imperialists lined up on one side and that if they were defeated, this would really be the war to end all wars. So they joined up. And do you know who the first American to win the French Cross of Honor was? Henry Johnson. A black man. While our armies were still segregated, he went and fought in the French ranks and the French recognized his nobility. Henry Johnson. A black man.

"We had segregated units in the Civil War. In the First World War. In the Second World War. In Korea. But that's when it changed, in Korea. Not that long ago, really." He pauses, and reaches for something more. "That's why we study history. To remember, to remember that all these things, these dangers—Hitler, segregation—it's all not that long ago. And look at Bosnia—not that far from us, right now." The Italian student, sitting next to Marsha, says "History repeats itself." Marsha, whose head is on her desk, has been paying attention nonetheless. She calls out loudly, "We need to WAKE UP. WAKE UP." Her friend, the Italian girl, is stroking Marsha's hair, a sign of intimacy that schoolgirls have managed to preserve. But for a white girl to stroke a black girl's hair like that, with such casual tenderness in such a public place, is rare, and touching. Segregation, as Murphy said, was not that long ago; that grown men and women–teachers–are surprised by a white girl's tenderness to a black girl in a public school in 1994 is proof.

"Quickly, before you go, close your books." Those few who had their heavy copies of *Rise of the American Nation* open now close them. Murphy holds up a copy of the *Lynn Item*. "Is there anybody here who didn't talk about this today?" The students murmur, but they've all been talking about the shooting at Classical. "Does it make you nervous?" "It happens everywhere," one student says. "It doesn't help public relations to see this thing in the paper, on the news. It's terrible, terrible, but it's no bigger than all the good things here, I think," Murphy says. No response, but Murphy feels that the class is with him. "If you go to work today, or out with people who aren't from Lynn, and they ask you about this, you might want to say, 'Yeah, it's a terrible thing, but you might want to know that in my school, we get along fine, even though it doesn't make the papers.' That's your job, to say that." The kids file out, and Bill Murphy stands alone in his classroom.

He doesn't really like being alone there. "I'm addicted to the kids. I don't like quiet places. If I could, I'd be in the classroom with every seat filled five days a week, every week of the year, teaching from eight in the morning till five at night." He looks around the room, back and forth, up and down. "You know, the acoustics here are terrible. I can hardly hear these kids when they speak, if I'm at the front of the room. But of course, when this place was built, the kids didn't speak. They just listened and wrote things down. Same when I was here." Murphy graduated from Lynn English in 1965. "When I was a student, they had hall monitors–kids with A averages–who walked around the halls all day and wrote down your name if you talked. There was no talking in the halls, none at all. Silence.

"I grew up here in Lynn, on Phillips Avenue, a nice place. You know one big difference between then and now? There were lots of teachers who lived in Lynn back then. Guys who taught in the Lynn schools owned nice houses in town. I'd see Jim Powers, my seventh-grade math teacher, with Mr. Baldwin and Mr. Gunn down at O'Connor's restaurant, drinking. I'd see teachers walking in the park on a Saturday, or driving through town, or out shopping. They lived right here, and they lived well on the teacher's salary back then. Not today. Most of us live in other towns now, and many, many work other jobs, too, just to have enough money to pay the mortgage. That affects the feeling of the town; now the typical teacher gets in the car at the end of the day, and the city of Lynn won't see that teacher until the next workday starts. And you can't really blame the teachers for that. They have families, most of the teachers, and they want to give their families what I had in Lynn thirty years ago, and I'm not sure they could find it anymore bringing up their kids in Lynn.

"When I was a kid, there were seven or eight movie theaters in Lynn. Now there are none. I remember going to the Warner theater right downtown, we could walk down there on the railroad tracks, no fear at all, no question that you didn't want to walk on the tracks because it was isolated. That's what made it fun. We walked down to the Warner one day and saw *Run Silent, Run Deep*, a World War Two submarine picture with Burt Lancaster. Boy, I'll never forget that. And there was a drive-in on the Lynnway, too. Now what's there? Car lots. Discount stores.

"Mostly what we did as kids was we played ball, all day, all night. Right there in the street, we'd play football for hours. We never hung out, just standing around. That's one thing I can't understand about the kids today, they hang out all the time, doing nothing. We just played all day long, running from the morning till night. Maybe at seven-thirty, when it started to get dark, we'd stand still and drink a tonic before we went in, but that was it.

"Then I went off to college, knowing right from the start that I'd be a teacher. I figured I'd wind up in some other town, not because I wanted to leave Lynn, but because there could only be so many jobs in any given school system. And the other towns nearby, they weren't so different from Lynn anyway; there wasn't so much of a division of the good towns from big bad Lynn as there is now. When I graduated, I went up and down Route 1A, up to Newburyport, to Hamilton, in all the towns, applying for teaching jobs. I didn't get anything, so I finally went over to Lynn and the deputy superintendent at the time offered me a job right away, and he said 'Why didn't you try us first? Why didn't you come to your hometown first?' And I didn't really have an answer. I just didn't think of it.

"So I started teaching here, found a place to live, and I was happy. I loved teaching. In 1978 I moved out, not to get away from the town, but just because I needed to find a new place, and I happened to find one in Salem. It was just a matter of chance. Then from Salem, I got married and we moved to Peabody, but again it wasn't to avoid Lynn, not then. It *would* be the case today, but it wasn't then."

Murphy and his wife had three children, but recently they divorced. "It's been terrible. Our own little Vietnam." Now he's living in Danvers, in an apartment complex near the North Shore Mall. "You know what's interesting, though, about the difference between all these towns? My daughter, who goes to the high school in Peabody, wanted to come to Lynn English, through the school choice program. She's heard me talk about how fascinating the mixture of kids is, how rich the experience here is in some ways, and we applied for her to come here through school choice. If the available slots hadn't been filled, she'd be here now. In Peabody, she's going to school almost entirely with white kids, and she misses the kind of education that happens with the mix of the black, Hispanic, and Cambodian kids, the Russian kids, the others. I understand what she was thinking. She's right in a lot of ways."

The hallways are noisy now, as classes change at English High. Inside any classroom a minute or two before a new class period begins, the noise is almost shocking. This might be another trick of the acoustics, though; the classrooms actually seem to draw noise in from the hallways.

After school, the cafeteria is still not quiet. Students gather and talk, walk by on the way to the gym or a club meeting or on the way home. Joe, the teacher's aide, is sitting alone, waiting for someone. He's been deeply affected by the shooting at Classical. "The kid who was killed? I knew him. He was over my house all the time. He was my sister's friend. She was there, right there in the pizza place. I mean, if he had fell backwards instead of forwards, she would have caught him, that's how close she was.

"But I'm not saying I'm any better than he was. I mean, I'm living a clean life now, I'm past that shit, but there was a time, boy, there was a time. When I was a student at Classical, I'd stay out of class and go to the bathroom. That's where you went to show your piece. You go there, pull out your pistol, show it around. Maybe you have somebody else's piece in your hand, feeling how heavy it feels. Feels good. Yes it does."

Sandy comes over to join Joe, and soon, Jay is there too. "I'll tell you what it is," Sandy says. "It's what you choose. These two guys were in the life, man, that's why they were killed. Everybody knows that, everybody knows it wasn't just some necklace or over some girl. Maybe that was like the last straw, you know, but these were people who lived hard. Did they go to school? Sometimes, not much. Did they hang out? Yes. Did they have guns? Now I don't know these boys that they did or they didn't but I'm telling you, somewhere, they had guns. This was the kind of guys they were, so it wasn't such a surprise, really. It was a bad thing, but it was their thing."

Jay shakes his head. He doesn't like what Sandy's just said. "Maybe, maybe not. I don't know. I don't think so. You pick up the gun because you got to. You feel a big need, it's a choice to keep your head above the water, you know. A person could carry, but they could be the weakest person on earth. But when they carry, they have the biggest heart in the world. Sometimes you need that big heart, man."

What, exactly, does Jay fear enough to make him carry a gun? Jay shakes his head, looking down. He doesn't want to answer. Joe says, "the only fear I have is jail. I'm clean now cause that's where I'm *not* going." Jay picks his head back up. Yes, he says, "that's it. That's the lesson."

Jay and Joe have said that at one point or another, they've had guns. Sandy hasn't volunteered anything. "My mother," he says now, "if I get arrested, she says the first time, she's gonna come down and get me. The second time, no. The second time, she's gonna start to forget who I ever was."

Sandy says he worries about three temptations in his life. Skipping school ("Could I have a better day somewhere else? No question about that one. Go to somebody's house, find a girl, have a party. Every day, that's where I could be."). Hanging out late ("My parents don't like it if I come in at two or three in the morning. They won't drag me in, but they say they're disappointed in me. I feel that. I want to do the right thing. Out late's when the worst shit happens, too. I like the idea of being in early. But out late's where the life is best, you know? It's an easy choice, but it's a hard thing to actually do.") His third temptation, he says, is "making money." Dealing drugs. "Right down from the street from my house, at La Grange Terrace. That's where it is. I know who, how much, when and where. It's maybe a couple hundred bucks in a good day selling weed." Sandy won't admit to selling or using any drugs other than marijuana. "I done it. I worked for the weed, make my money the selling way. It wasn't hard. I like having the money. Money, money, money. That's good. I like it. But I don't like being a dealer. It don't feel good. It's all black teens doing the work, too, but it's run by a white guy. That's hard to be part of." Jay also says he has sold drugs at La Grange Terrace. But he won't talk about it.

Jay says there's just one temptation in his life: violence. He's struggling to stay on track, to keep coming back to school every day, and to resist the urge that bubbles up now and then, the urge to beat someone's head in. "The other day," he says, offering a case in point, "there was tacos for lunch in the cafeteria. I got a bad stomach, I can't take that kind of food, so I was gonna go out, buy a sandwich. This teacher, she was acting vice-principal, 'cause the others were out somewhere. She sees me walking out, like ten minutes after the lunch started, she said I couldn't go out. I asked her real nice, told her my stomach couldn't take those tacos. She said no. I said, 'Well, I've got to do something for myself. You say no, all right.' And I kept walking over to my locker to get my coat. She saw me and said, 'I'll suspend you.' I just kept going. Later, I got back, I saw her in the hall and she said I'd get a five-day suspension. Goddamn. There's no reason for that. I thought I was gonna just snatch up on her right there, just reach out and grab her fucking neck. That's what I worry about, that I'll do that to a teacher."

Jay works at getting in to school regularly, keeping his temper steady, doing his school work. He plays basketball and football, and worries that if he's out too many days or if his grades slip, he'll lose his eligibility to play. After two years in school here, he still hasn't found a teacher he can talk to outside of class, talk about his life, his worries. Does it matter to him that almost every teacher at English is white? "Yes it does. It does. They look at me, I don't know what they think. But I can see a fear sometimes that's because these are white people and I'm black. Yes, that matters to me."

Grady comes by the cafeteria, listens in on the conversation, and says, "Could you imagine what everybody in this town would be saying if those two boys who got shot at Classical were white, but the guy who shot them was black? Damn, they'd put handcuffs on every nigger in this school." Sandy and Jay laugh, and say "That's right, that's right." Joe doesn't laugh, but he agrees, too. Joe says, "That'd be the end of the quiet days at English High School. Every asshole driving by'd be throwing goddamn rocks and bottles. Every white kid's parents would be coming down to meetings, they'd say what are we gonna do about those colored boys. Goddamn, they throw a bottle at me, that's the end of it. That's the end.

"You know there's fighting, there's shooting, usually it's one black man hurting another. You know that's the way it is right here. Sometimes there's fights between the blacks and the Spanish in Lynn. But the white people are separated, and a lot of them, not all of them but a lot of them, they're afraid of us, and I think lots of blacks are afraid of the white people. But just one thing happens, one stupid white kid says the wrong word, throws a bottle at me, the peace is gone. Right now we're fighting each other because we're angry, but you know we ain't angry at ourselves. There's a lot more anger here to go around, a lot more. This school does a good job, I'll say that and I'm being straight. I think Patuleia does a good job, he tries to do right. But he will never give me or Sandy or Jay what we need at the hard times, because he's a white man. God made him that way, and you just look at the man, he's white all the way through. There are things he won't be able to do for me or for half the people in this school. When he goes to sleep in his bed tonight and he says to himself, how am I gonna keep my school safe so there's no shooting, how am I gonna keep those angry black men away from my kids, he's never gonna find the answer to that question. He locked up the doors—you gotta ring the bell to get in if you're five minutes late. That's not gonna keep the angry black men out. He puts the monitors in the hall. That's not gonna keep the angry black men out either. Because they're already in. Here they are. And he can't stop a bullet in this school, or outside it. I like the man. He's working hard, and I give him respect for that. But there's only one thing that's gonna stop a bullet in this school, and that's a black man. That's a hard lesson, and I don't think he's figured that one out yet."

After the others have left, Sandy lingers. He says that when he heard about the shooting, the first thing he thought was that Jay was involved. "He's been good for a couple of weeks, but I thought, 'Goddamn, he shot somebody.' I didn't think he *got* shot, he's not that type of kid, but I thought he was the one who would pull the trigger. Now I'm thinking I have to think better thoughts about my man, you know? Like I did him wrong thinking about that. But I tell you, if it is him next time, I won't be surprised. I still gonna think it if someone says there's a shooting. I'm still watching this boy, thinking maybe I can pull him back from where he's going." Sandy looks sad, assaulted by the futility of his task. "I'm trying. I'm trying, but I don't know. I can look at this boy and I know the end of the story already." Meanwhile, Jay is already outside, joking and laughing with Joe, waiting for Sandy to join them.

"Am I over all that shit?" Jay asks later. "I say yes, I'm done with trouble. But you know, the world tells you what you got to do sometimes. I'm over it if the world lets me be in peace. Today, it's peace. But I won't make a promise for tomorrow, 'cause tomorrow ain't here yet, is it?"

The next day, after lunch, a young woman in her last year at English lowers her voice to say that she doesn't feel entirely safe in the school. "Some of the people here, I can tell they look at me when I walk by, because I wear nice clothes and I have a certain image, you know? I get worried. They look at me and they're thinking, 'There goes that white girl.' It makes me nervous. I think they bring too many problems to school with them, and maybe the school would be better off without them. But would I say there's racial problems? No, I wouldn't. We get along. I don't see too many of them being angry; they keep that apart from the regular life here. I just get a little worried, you know? I just wonder, what are they thinking?" Her friend, who has been listening, is less delicate: "I don't have a problem with black people. If you behave yourself, and you treat people with respect, I don't have any problem with you. But there's a difference between black people and niggers, you understand? Niggers I don't have any use for. Niggers I have a problem with. But not all blacks are niggers. Lots of the people here I respect. They don't treat me with ignorance, so they're not niggers and I have no problems with them. With them, there's no racial issue. But the others, the niggers, they bring the racial problem with them. They *are* the racial problem."

One of the two black teachers at English High, Jane Turner teaches English, mostly lower-skill-level classes. Her classroom opens onto the cafeteria, and on the way to visit her, I bump into the soccer coach. He's talking with a student who's backing away from him, trying to take his place in a rushing throng headed out of the cafeteria, but the coach won't let him go so easily. "So you'll come? You'll come? Definitely? Tonight at six?" Yes, yes, the student says, he'll be there. He turns quickly and then he is gone. "This kid," the coach says, "you see him, you think: a big black kid, he must be violent. But he's the salt of the earth. Gentle, always ready to spend more time here helping out. Surprising sometimes, what you can get from these kids."

Jane Turner's Career English 9 is the lowest-level English class at the school, nominally for future clerical workers. In fact, the class is a catch basin for the students judged unable to do the work of the college-track or honors classes. Some of the students are in special education programs, having been diagnosed with learning disabilities; others are recent arrivals from Haiti or the Dominican Republic, who have never attended English-language schools before; and some are just weak students with no obvious reasons for their poor performance. To sit and watch these students is often to feel sad—they are so far behind, they need so much attention, and there is so little available. But sometimes, they surprise you: a word, or maybe a look, of the purest intelligence.

Turner comes in late. Her first question: "Does anyone have gum?" None of the thirteen students confess, but Turner looks about shrewdly, not fooled for a minute. She settles in at her desk while the students chat quietly, or sit in silence and discomfort, the more common alternative. One by one, she calls students up to her desk to inspect homework. "Check out the Impact books while I'm checking homework," she calls out to the class, not lifting her eyes from the ledger in front of her on her desk. A girl calls out, "I did it already." Turner looks up. "Well," she says, with exaggerated patience and a cold smile, "did you do *all* the questions?" "No." "Well, do *all* of them." She returns to the book in front of her, then calls out a student's name and begins looking over his homework book. "Cora," she says loudly, without looking up, "you have gum. I said please get rid of it." Cora goes to the garbage can along the front wall and says something under her breath as she passes Turner's desk. "Don't speak Spanish," Turner says, matter-of-factly.

Four mismatched teachers' desks line the front wall of Turner's classroom. Piles of books and blue plastic organizing trays and papers and green and brown loose-leaf binders sit in heaps spread across all four. A small clear space at the center of Turner's desk gives her enough room to spread out the day's tools: a reader, a grade ledger, her book bag. "What was the homework," one boy asks his neighbor in a quiet voice. Without looking up, Turner answers: "To write sentences." She's almost done calling the students up for homework checking, but she hears one girl, Beth, chatting too loudly with Cora, who sits next to her. Again without looking up: "Beth, your mouth is open and sounds are coming out." Beth is quickly silent, but she and Cora want badly to laugh. Turner impresses them. She's tough—she sees without looking up; hears the quietest voice. She's a real teacher.

Done with the homework, Turner finally raises her head and says to the class, "We have a new student. Herman is from Haiti." She looks over to a slim black boy, and the others follow her gaze. Herman sits uncomfortably; he stares at his shoes, glancing up once or twice to take in the class and Miss Turner, though his eyes dart back down to his shoes whenever his gaze is met. The other students sit with their books open, though most of them look away—out the windows looking over the snow-covered football field, out the other set of windows, looking into the cafeteria, or they rummage quietly through their book bags, whisper to each other, draw inky spots on their sneakers. Cora and Beth are talking to each other, a little louder than the other students. Turner lets the hum of conversation and

private activity keep on as she calls one sullen-looking girl up
to her desk. "Sweetheart," she says quietly, "is something wrong?
Can I help?" The girl shakes her head no. "No? Then don't
take it out on me, please." The girl goes back to her seat.

"Sweetheart," Turner says loudly in Cora's direction, "my
ears are very attuned to little whiny voices." She pauses, lets
her message sink in. Then she addresses the class: "Close your
books. Tell me, what is the title of the story we're reading?"
Two tentative voices, one near the front and one near the back,
speak in unsure unison—"All Summer in a Day." "That's right,
'All Summer in a Day,' by Ray Bradbury. And who is the main
character in this book?" Cora calls out, "Margaret." Turner
says, "Yes. Margaret." She pauses though, and then says "Actually, it's Margot—Mar-*go*." "Why is there a *t*, then," Cora asks.
"It's a French name or something, I think," Turner says. Tuner
works to elicit the story-line from her students, and slowly they
articulate the plot—an Earth girl on Venus is locked in a closet
by her Venusian playmates as revenge for her superior attitude. "How was she when she got out of the closet," Turner
asks. A girl in front says, "They don't say." "Yes," Turner says,
"that's important. Look at what they don't say as well as what
they do say. Those things left unsaid are very important too."
Turner looks at Cora, but Cora seems lost—she's flipping
though her book, looking for the right page. Turner tells her
the page number in Spanish, and Cora corrects her pronun-
ciation. "Don't tell me about Spanish," Turner says, "I know
more about your language than you do." Her tone is mocking,
but playful, too, and Cora takes it with a small laugh. Turner
reads one of the reading comprehension questions in the book:
The events of the story suggest that Margot will a) never adjust, b) get even, c) make friends. Someone—a girl; the boys
don't seem to speak—calls out c. "What makes you say c," Turner
asks. "Why would anyone want to make friends with little brats
who lock her in a closet?" She doesn't get an answer, and goes
on to another question. "What does Margot look like?" No response. Turner says, quietly, "Blond, pale—" Someone calls out
"like me" and everyone laughs; no one in this classroom is
blond and pale. "She's even white haired. No one here is white
haired yet." She turns back to the multiple choice question—
what will happen to Margot? Will she make friends? The stu-

dents like the simplicity of the question; they relate to it. They call out a and b and c, they talk back and forth with Turner and among themselves, trying to figure it out.

Then Turner moves to the book's True or False statements. The first: Although the story takes place on a different planet, the children behave pretty much as children on Earth do. The class responds with a muttering chorus of Yeses and Trues. Turner goes on with the next statement: They treat Margot differently because she's from somewhere else. The answer, again, is yes. "Any similarities to this school here?" Turner asks. Some Yeses and some Nos. Four of the thirteen students in class are black, including Herman, the new student from Haiti. They are all silent. The three Hispanic students in class, including Cora, are also quiet. Two girls in the front row take up the issue: "Like maybe how you dress, or your weight," one says; "If you're from Russia or something," says the other.

Turner moves to another question in the book: Where does Margot want to go? "Ohio." Turner turns toward the second voice, pleased. "Good baby," she coos to the girl. Cora and her friend are talking again, in Spanish, and Turner hears Cora say *coño*—a common Spanish vulgarism for female anatomy. Turner leaps and, with a burst of energy, shouts "Oh! Oh! Oh!" The class is stunned, though Cora and her friend laugh nervously. "Did I tell you yesterday? Should I give you another piece of paper?" The class call out "yes" with great pleasure— they want more punishments. "How many hundred more times do you have to write out 'I will not say hmmm-hmmm'?" Cora's grin is sheepish, but genuine—she's enjoying the attention, and Turner, everyone can see, is not really mad.

Turner takes a big breath, smiles again, and turns back to the text. "What's the weather like? Find me a sentence about the weather on Venus. Someone?" Bob, a lanky Hispanic boy in drooping yellow jeans, raises his hand, finds the sentence, and reads it out with fluency and grace. "Beautiful, Bob," Turner says, as surprised as everyone else by this silent boy's intelligence. Bob smiles and straightens up in his chair.

"Vocabulary!" Turner calls out. "Resilient. What does it mean?" No answers. Turner looks around the room. "If I take Nicole," she says, "if I take her out and start punching her and punching her and saying I'm sick of you talking in my class and I'm sick of you never doing my homework"—by this point Nicole's eyes are open wide; Turner walks toward her—"and punching you and punching you"—Turner illustrates by banging her on the shoulder—"and then the next day she comes back, still talking, still not doing her homework, she's not sitting at home crying saying 'she hit me, she hit me,' she *don't care*, she's *resilient*."

A bell rings—class is over. On her way out, Cora's friend Ann asks Turner "How do I use 'nonchalantly'?" "If I hit Chris," Turner says to illustrate, grabbing a totally uncomprehending boy, but before she can continue, Ann rescues Chris: "Chris doesn't get it," she says, grabbing his cheek and giving him the kind of pinch one expects only from middle-aged aunts. "Ouch!" he says. Turner makes a face at Ann, who defends herself: "What? I was only giving him a *dooge*."

Walking out from Turner's classroom into the cafeteria, the students are surprised by the emptiness—just a few kids squeezing through the exit doors, trailing the crowds already in the hallways heading out of the building. One of the vice-principals calls out to Turner's confused students, "Everybody out! Quickly, calmly, everybody out. Evacuate." They all run to the exit. "No running!" he says, but it's useless—the students are already gone in a blur. Outside, the sun shines on the assembled student body, though the air is cold and some kids try to get into the building to retrieve coats from their lockers. But a handful of teachers stand about twenty feet in front of the building and tell the students to stay back; in front of them, five fire trucks form a crescent. No one gets past the fire trucks. At first, everyone wonders why they've been put out. Then word spreads—there's been a fire. Smoke begins to seep out of a rear door, and then more smoke rises from the roof over the school auditorium. After about half an hour—and a few scuffles, and a steady stream of departees from the rear end of the crowd—school is officially canceled for the day. Some students remain near the school anyway, with no better place to go.

The police department later reports that a 15-year-old student has been caught and charged with arson. Patuleia expels him, and he is eventually turned over to the Massachusetts Department of Social Services and placed in a treatment program for youthful arsonists. "He was a pyromaniac," a Lynn

Police spokesman says later. "Nothing to do with the school. He could have done this anytime, any place."

Two years earlier, the firestarter might not have been expelled, or even caught. The school was going though a year and a half without a real principal, and no one was making the hard decisions, like whether or not to expel a student. English High *had* had a strong principal, Al Tagney, for years, but when he retired, the Lynn school committee just wasn't prepared to find a permanent replacement right away. "Al Tagney was a wonderful principal, a great educator," says a former English High teacher who still sees him every so often. "But the cuts were getting to him. Every year, he had to run fewer courses, even though he had more students. Every year, he had more problems coming to him uninvited. He felt like he was no longer in control. It really affected him. If you cared about the man, in those last couple of years, you worried about him. Now, though, he's happy as a clam. Mostly, he plays golf."

Others remember him less generously, saying that in the old days of Lynn English, Tagney was a good leader, but that he couldn't accept change. "I remember him as the basketball coach when I was a student," Bill Murphy says. "Even then, you could see the rigidity, the stiffness. In every bone, every muscle, you could see the tension in this man. And when I began teaching here, I never saw him. He just stayed in his office. Teachers called it 'The Bunker.' He didn't like what was going on in the school, so he isolated himself from it all. He gave up, but he stayed on anyway. Only after a few years of isolation did he retire. Some people here say that's part of the reason the building was allowed to deteriorate so. They wanted to get Tagney out, but he was hanging on, so they made things as unpleasant as possible for him here. Don't fix this, don't fund that, and sooner or later he'll give up, he'll come out of the bunker."

After Tagney left, a series of temporary principals came through the building, and discipline fell apart. Most lunch hours were interrupted by fights; teachers weren't supervised or given much support; no one had a plan for dealing with the big changes sweeping through the building. Or almost no one.

Ken Curtis, the assistant principal Patuleia squeezed out in his first months as principal, says he is happy now as vice-principal at one of Lynn's junior high schools. He says he doesn't want anything more than he's got now; he doesn't want to be a principal. Not anymore, at least. "When we were in a period of transition, of disorder," Curtis says, "back then I thought English needed direction. I put in a bid for the position of principal, and I presented a plan for change to the school committee. I proposed setting up three different schools inside English. On the third floor, we would run a college prep school. On the second floor, a business school. On the first floor, a school for immigrants. The immigrants could see the others, and they could participate in the other activities as they became able to, but they wouldn't just be thrown in to fail as they are now." The committee rejected Curtis's plan. Instead, they tapped Patuleia to take over. Curtis was left in place as vice-principal, but not for long.

"Once he was gone," Patuleia relates, "the core of old-time teachers who resented me began to soften. They began to see that I had some support in the superintendent's office, and that I was in for the long haul. They weren't going to scare me by being difficult. I would play by the rules. I would be forgiving, I would give anyone who played fair a break, but what you did when you went about your job as a teacher in my school would be public, not private. What you said to your students, whether you came to the important meetings, what you had to say to me in public, all these things would be remembered, and if you acted unprofessionally, if you played games, if you didn't do your job, it would matter. That hadn't always been the case in this school, but with Curtis leaving, lots of others got the message that from now on, the work mattered. Not just how long you'd been in the building or how many friends you had, but the kind of work you do every day, in the classroom with the kids and as part of a team that makes the school operate. They got shook up. They said to themselves, 'We'd better do our jobs. They lopped off a v.p., they'll go after anyone.'

"But that's only half the story. I need these people to be on my side, even if they hate me. I need them to come in and do the work, to be as fair as they can be to the students, and I know I'm not going to get that by making them afraid.

"Just a couple of months ago, you know what I did? I put together a staff recognition night. We got NYNEX to pick up part of the tab, had a big dinner and gave out awards to every-one teaching here with thirty years or more as a teacher. It was great. Of course at first, when I started talking about doing this, a couple of people said, 'Well, let's do it as part of a lunch during an in-service training day,' or 'let's tack it on the end of some meeting.' Just typical, typical blue-collar, small-minded stuff. I said no, this has got to be special. So we did it right, and it was the Academy Awards for these people, something they'll never forget. They were overwhelmed. Twenty-seven teachers got awards—beautiful engraved golden apples, certifi-cates from the Department of Education, and a coupon for dinner for two at another restaurant. Everyone who'd been sitting on the fence jumped right over to my side after that. One man, the hardest case in the building, the guy who gave me that first tour, trying to scare me away, he came to me the next day, practically with tears in his eyes, to thank me.

"So even with the hard cases, the old-timers, I'm making my way. Things are coming together. And then I've got to sit down at the end of the year and see how many new people I can hire. That's the big payoff. I'll have more than ten new teachers whom I've hired in the building by next September, and these are people I can choose myself—professional, energetic people. My people. Every year, more and more of them. That's how I'll win this battle, by hanging in longer than anyone who wants to fight me, any kid, any teacher. Every year I stay here, my roots go deeper and the school becomes more and more *my* school."

One teacher Patuleia has already won over is a bilingual English teacher, a woman with six years in the building but without any hesitation in her support for the new principal. "There's a positive feeling here that there hadn't been in place for a long time. There's a direction. We don't seem stagnant anymore." She's less optimistic about her students. "Most of them, when I think about where they might be in ten years, it's not good. It's not what I'd want for my own children. A lot of them graduate and then take more ESL classes at the commu-nity college, but what kind of jobs can they get really? Domes-tic work, that's still something they can find, but I'm not happy as their teacher to think that I'm training them to be maids. And service work, low-paying jobs cleaning up or taking or-ders. The new immigrants will probably do better in the long run, once they've mastered English, but the ones here who've been here for ten years already and don't have a good grasp of the language, you wonder how far they'll be able to go." Unlike many bilingual teachers, she wasn't brought up in a Spanish-speaking home. By background, she's hardly distinguishable from other teachers at Lynn English—not very old, not very young, white, middle-class. One thing does mark her as different, though: in 1975, she joined the Peace Corps and spent two years in South America. Still, she knows her students don't reap a great deal from her idealism, or whatever is left of it nineteen years later. "They've got to have someone who's really street smart working for them, pushing them and helping in the transition to work, or to whatever else they might do once their time here is over. And there's nobody here like that. They need that kind of advocate." Thinking over the arc of years between the Peace Corps and Lynn English, she says, "I've changed a great deal since those early years. I think I have more—the big lesson is, you're all right, you're O.K., you can succeed. That's what the years in between have borne out for me." She sits quietly, thinking over what she has said. I wonder if the same lesson will follow for her students, too.

Chapter Three

Fingers and Signs and Moons

Joe Patuleia is usually the first to arrive at school every morning, around six AM, though twice a week he gets in by five-
thirty to play a six o'clock basketball game with a handful of
students and teachers. He plays serious ball, passing straight
cannon shots into his teammates' bellies, and he can hit baskets with remarkable fluency. Still, he is not young, and not
tall, and not slim. He's outclassed by the sleek youths who come
to play with him. He showers in his office—one corner holds a
private bathroom, the walls still dark green, the color his whole
office wore until eighteen months of nagging paid off and the
janitors repainted, off-white. Now, sitting at his claw-footed
partners' desk in the middle of his large room, Patuleia looks
more like an energetic CEO than the civil-service green would
ever have allowed.

By seven AM, others are trickling in, a few teachers but mostly
students, some for a free breakfast in the cafeteria, some to sit
and finish homework, and some to hang out with their friends
and claim a bit of space in the hallways or the cafeteria, safe
from the monitors until homeroom at eight.

Francisco Grullon supervises the cafeteria every morning.
He's been teaching at English High for eight years, and is one
of only two Hispanic teachers at the school. His last period is
always free, part of the deal he made in exchange for starting
each schoolday with cafeteria duty at seven. His English is
heavily accented, and some of the other teachers make little
effort to hide their scorn. "I'd come in at seven, no problem, if
you let me go home at one o'clock," says one coach. "Why's he
the one with that deal? I'll tell you why—it's his bonus for be-

ing Spanish. So, no, I don't like that. I can't even understand what the man says half the time. You can't tell me he's a good role model for the kids, talking like that." Grullon must be aware of tension. He dresses almost too well—a suit every day, but most of his suits are a size too large, cuffs riding up to his palms as he stands at ease, looking over the morning cafeteria crowd, and he seems nervous talking to most other teachers.

Massachusetts has hired relatively few teachers in the past five years; the state budget has been shrinking, and education hasn't been spared. Most teachers count themselves lucky to have their jobs, and many can name friends who have been trying to get teaching jobs for months, and in some cases, years. English and social studies teachers are particularly superfluous these days. Math and science teachers have it a little easier, but hardly any schools go out recruiting. One small ad in the *Boston Globe* brings in between twenty and two hundred applications for a single vacancy. Except for bilingual teachers. State and federal mandates demand that schools with a substantial number of students who don't speak English at home hire certified bilingual teachers, who can teach a subject in both English and another language. Students from Spanish-speaking homes might be taught biology or American history in Spanish while they also take English language classes. But bilingual teachers are hard to find, so schools compete for them, and a man like Francisco Grullon seems to have it easy. Some teachers think that there is something unfair about rewarding Grullon for his fluency in Spanish when he *is*, as they say, Spanish.

Grullon strolls around the cafeteria at seven-thirty, talking to the Dominican and Central American kids. "I can understand them. They'll tell me if they have a problem. If I didn't speak Spanish, no, I don't think they would. And the Russian kids, too," he says, pointing to a table full of muscular boys in tailored slacks and tight T-shirts—they look like 1950s juvenile delinquents. Like most of the Dominican and Central American students at English High, the Russian students are recent immigrants, and many don't speak English well. But they want nothing to do with the Spanish-speakers. Their chauvinism is obvious. "These Spanish kids, they're not so smart. I don't know—maybe their parents don't care, maybe they just don't have it, you know?" says one Russian boy, tapping his temple. "They just don't have ability."

So what makes Grullon think he can reach them? He pulls one Russian boy away from his friends. Quietly, Grullon asks him a question in Russian. They talk for a few minutes, and then Grullon heads over to another table. "I'm the only one who speaks Russian. The only teacher in the school." He smiles, proud of this. "They like that." ("He speaks Russian?" one teacher asks, genuinely surprised. "Where'd he learn Russian?")

By eight, the cafeteria has begun emptying out. The students head to their homerooms, where their teachers will take attendance. Morning announcements come over the public address system, and through the televisions mounted on the front wall of each classroom. The TVs came from Whittle Communications, for free. In many of the classrooms at English High, amid mismatched chairs and desks, cracked bulletin boards and leaky ceilings, a spiffy color set stands out as the only new thing—in fact, the only remotely modern thing—to be seen. But they were not *entirely* free.

One classroom at English has been made over into a television production studio, presided over by Evan and the rest of the Television Club. In a small alcove at the rear of the room, a black box the size of a microwave oven sits on a table. It's the "Whittle Box." In the middle of the night, a satellite beams about ten minutes of news programming into the box. During homeroom, all the televisions turn on automatically, and the news program, complete with commercials, plays. This is Whittle Communications' nationwide business venture: Channel One TV. Whittle bought the television sets and a range of video equipment for the school in exchange for two promises. First, the school had to promise that the news and commercials would be aired every day on those television sets. Second, they had to promise that while the Channel One show is on, teachers won't compete with the TVs—they'll just direct the students to watch the sets.

In Bill Murphy's class, unlike most others, the television has been mounted on a back wall. At 8:00, Murphy himself has not yet arrived, but five students sit in a corner, chatting. More kids come in, Murphy himself arrives, and at 8:08, the television turns itself on. Some students watch; most don't. The

Channel One anchors are high school students, but they don't look like the students watching (or not watching) them at English—they look so clean, so coordinated, so sure. Their scripted remarks are perfect. At English, every word comes with its attendant doubt, its slouch, its backward glance and hopeful shrug. On Channel One, the kids seem always to be at the right place at the right time, knowing everything they need to know. The first story this morning is about school choice. A thirty-second clip of Secretary of Education Riley holds no one's attention, but an on-the-scene interview with students at a school in Cerritos, California (introduced by the young anchor as "a Channel One school in Cerritos, California"), draws in a couple of Murphy's homeroom students. They listen as mostly Chicano students in Cerritos talk about the different schools they can choose from—some with special art programs, some with special sports and physiology programs. "Damn. California's nice," one student says. A longer feature on a Fox television show follows, and then a piece on young professional black women. Still, most of the students in the room talk, rush to finish homework, or just roll their heads with a practiced sense of boredom. Before Channel One ends, Murphy starts calling the roll.

The first couple of students whose names he calls are present. Then, five in a row are absent. "Absent, Absent, Absent," Murphy says, not really disappointed—this is par for the course. He reads another name. "Absent." Then two who are present, then another absent. Present. Present. Then another name, another absent: "He's MIA," Murphy says, then more names, a few present, about as many not. Murphy starts to play: "Absent. . . . MIA. . . MIA. . . POW. . .Traded to the Bruins."

After Channel One ends its broadcast, the screen goes blank for a moment, and then the local news comes on, the student-run morning show produced by Evan. It starts with a montage—a shot of the school on a sunny day, an incongruous long shot of a young woman playing tennis, a quick scene from a school play, kids goofing in the halls, then a young woman behind an anchor's desk begins reading the top story: police yesterday confiscated a shotgun from a merchant near school. "And now Michelle has the club news. Michelle?" The camera cuts to Michelle, and she reads off the list of club meetings for the day. Then the weather: a toothy boy with pasty red hair stands in front of a colorful weather map—brown paint for land, blue paint for the ocean, cloud cutouts stuck on (another day, it might be cutout snowflakes, or raindrops). The news ends with a sports report. The footage comes from a basketball game the night before. English lost, but the abrupt action is exciting—real exertion on the screen, bodies flashing past, a three-point basket sunk. And with that the news is over. A bell rings, and everyone squeezes out into the hall, off to the first class of the day.

Evan has his first two periods free. Officially, he is assigned to work with Mr. Brown, the television-production teacher, but Evan manages his own time in the mornings, preparing the next day's show. There's actually not much news to be gathered in the mornings. After-school sports events are the only challenging things to cover, and Patuleia doesn't allow anything controversial to air anyway (he confiscated Evan's tape of the Curtis walkout protesters before he could air any of it), so Evan doesn't do much investigating. The other news staple, aside from sports, is club news—meetings and projects to be announced—which tends to come in without much effort. So Evan spends his early hours mostly in the storeroom behind Mr. Brown's classroom, where the two VCRs and rows upon rows of old video tapes and even older, outdated video equipment are stored. He edits tape, meets with the half-dozen newscrew members who make up the TV Club, and sometimes walks the halls, talking to teachers, to the vice-principals, occasionally to Patuleia, establishing a presence, reminding everyone that he's always ready to air their announcements, to shoot some footage of an award or a performance or a new teacher.

Evan strolls past Mr. Murphy's door and peeks in. Murphy's showing a video about the Second World War, and there is Hitler on a podium, fierce and grim. "No teleprompter for him," Murphy says as Evan walks past. "Scary . . ." Down in the cafeteria, a pair of sleepy teachers supervise study hall. The students stare at their open books, some nod off, some actually take notes, looking thoughtful. Evan puts his arm around one boy, pulls him from his trance and reminds him of another TV Club meeting that day after school. "O.K., yeah, I'm with you," the boy says, sounding like he's just come out of a deep sleep. Evan crosses the cafeteria and passes a small glass display as he leaves. The display case is placed oddly high up—about eight feet up, above everyone's head. Inside is a dusty piece of posterboard with faded black ink spelling out a list of "Personality Traits": "Cooperation, Industry, Initiative, Loyalty, Neatness, Reliability." And then a question: "How do you stand?" Evan doesn't see it, doesn't even know it's there. No one I ask—no teacher, no student—recalls ever noticing it.

The lunch bell rings twice a day at English High. The cafeteria can only hold half the student body, so two lunch periods fill the early afternoon. As the last of the morning study halls nears the end of its dull hour in the cafeteria, a handful of white-aproned women emerge from a back storeroom *cum* kitchen, a cramped wood-paneled warren piled high with industrial drums of cranberry juice and cheese ravioli and tomato sauce. The women shuttle between the back room and the shining metal serving carts pushed together in a line along one cafeteria wall to form a serving counter, bringing out plates—and bowls—and buckets-full of sauces and sandwiches and soups, setting up the glass case that holds a hundred large, soft salty pretzels hanging on shiny metal hooks, kept warm by a large heating lamp below them. The janitors come in from a side room of their own, sliding rubber garbage cans across the room, one landing at the corner of each long dining table. The study hall students are jolted awake by garbage cans—big, red, smelly—spinning to a stop just inches from some of them. It must happen to them every day, but still most seem astounded by the intrusion, the raw energy of the janitors overriding their own forced idleness.

The janitors play a key role in the school, particularly in Patuleia's campaign to make the school safer. Like janitors in many big cities, Lynn school janitors work under a contract specifying that they work for the central school committee, not for the individual principals. (A friend in New York tells a story, which he swears is true. His children were going to a public grade school in Manhattan that had a lot of problems. The parents go after the principal, demanding changes, trying to get him to work harder to improve the school. In the heat of the parents' campaign, the principal resigns his job, and wangles an appointment as the building's janitor. He tells the parents he did it for two reasons: more freedom and more money. The Lynn school janitors seem to have a similarly good deal.)

Patuleia works hard to get his janitors on board, to get them feeling that things are changing, that English is becoming a better place. He gives them Christmas presents, pats them on the back, and asks them for advice whenever he can. Then around midyear something strange happens. His chief janitor comes into his office to complain about the teachers, saying that they're not helping keep the cafeteria clean, and his language becomes vulgar. Patuleia tells him that his language is unacceptable. "I just said, flat out, don't come in here talking about my teachers with that kind of language. He turned, walked out, and slammed my office door behind him. So I suspended him for a day. Now, one of the oldtimers on the staff here hears about this, and says, 'Well this is just Patuleia whipping us all down again,' and he takes up a collection for this janitor to replace his day's wage that he'll miss. This is the ultimate irony—I stand up for the teachers, tell the janitor he has to show them some respect, and this guy makes it out like I'm their enemy because I suspend the janitor. Well, soon enough the story gets around about what really happened, and this guy got egg on his face. He just looked dumb.

"The janitor, he's a good enough young guy. I think he figured something out from the suspension. He came closer to me when he got back. He took direction better. He started to accept me. And, you know, I'm the only principal in town who gives them Christmas gifts. I think I show them more respect than they can get anywhere else. He saw that too, over time, and now things are working all right." So now, at midday, the janitors really put some spin on those red rubber trash bins as they slide them out among sleepy study-hall students.

"Even though you're going down a good road, and your friends are on a bad road, don't think you're better than they are." Sandy is thinking about a few of his friends who have been getting in trouble lately. His parents, both ministers at Mount Olive Baptist Church in Lynn, have tried to teach him this kind of humility. His parents are a big presence in his life. "For example, I'm careful about who I'll take into my house,"

Sandy says. "Because my parents see my friends coming over the house sometimes with their hoods on and their hats and they say, 'Who is this, who is that,' but I bring good kids over only. You can't trust some of the others—they may be good to hang out with, maybe to get high with or whatever, but there are some kids I could have a good influence on who I still don't want inside my family's house." Sandy's friend David is always welcome, though. He is a distant cousin, and Sandy's parents know and like David's mother. They think of him as a fine young man.

David is a fair student. His grades probably won't win him admittance to a four-year college, but he has the intelligence to start with a two-year community college and to go on after that. In school, David is nondescript—not the smartest, not the dumbest. Not a problem. "I'm just a regular guy," he says, "trying to get away from the problems that are waiting for me. Trying to make some money to get away from the problems." As he sees them, the problems are about drugs and crime. Many of the boys he grew up with have left school. Some deal drugs at La Grange, some do crimes for a living, some live off their parents, sleeping all day, out all night. David can imagine where these young men will wind up, and he wants no part of that kind of future. But to keep on at school, he feels he needs some kind of reward, some taste of the stable life to come after he graduates and goes to college and starts a career. A little money now and then seems like reasonable compensation for staying in school, for being respectful most of the time, for choosing a good life instead of running with his hard friends. Like Sandy, David won't cut himself off from the toughest, hardest boys, but he's sure about his own fiber. Like Sandy, he knows, deep down, he's made of better stuff.

David does well at school when he has to—he'll show up for tests, and he'll usually pass them. He'll skip out sometimes, but not often enough to fail. He likes math more than English. He likes lunch more than math. "They leave you alone at lunch. Usually." But today he won't be there. The white gloom of a long, snowy winter is lifting, ice melting, and today there's a bit of sun. His breath won't steam in front of his face, which David takes as a sign of hope. He celebrates by skipping school.

Most days David walks a little less than a mile from predominantly black West Lynn to school. Lynn school planners of the 1920s could not have guessed that seventy years into its history, English High would lie in Lynn's neutral zone, the neighborhood that's not West Lynn, not Lynn Highlands, not-white Lynn, not-black Lynn, not-Latino Lynn. Unplanned, this accident of geography serves the school well; it is no one's natural turf, and offers most of its students a step away from the factions of their neighborhoods.

But David isn't going there today. Wearing a light leather jacket, shivering only a little and feeling the strong sun on his face and neck, he walks instead to the commuter-train station, where a cluster of buses idles under an overpass. He hops on one, drops in eighty-five cents, and claims a seat in the fur-thest-back row, his empty backpack planted beside him. The ride is quick—not south to Boston, where most travelers want to go at nine-thirty in the morning, but north, one town, two towns up, where David gets off along a busy road, not far from a strip mall with a K-mart, a supermarket, a discount mattress store, a pizza-place, a toy-store, and a pharmacy. The parking lot is big, several hundred spaces, but this early, only every fourth or fifth spot is taken. The pizza place is only now open-ing; crowds won't start until noon. So David waits. He strolls through the K-Mart. "They follow me, check up on me. If noth-ing else makes me want to cop something, that's enough. I'll do it just to say 'Fuck you, you worry so much about what I'll do then I just have to give you something to worry about, don't I?' Maybe take a baseball glove or some perfume or something." But not today. David spends about an hour walking from aisle to aisle, picking up some fishing rods, looking through maga-zines, trying out the lawn furniture set out on the white lino-leum floor.

Then he heads over to the pizza shop. It's about 11:30, the parking lot is almost half full, but David's still not ready yet, so he has a slice of pizza and an orange soda. He sits, looking out the plate-glass window at the cars. The sun is getting higher; glare bounces off the car windows. That's good. That will help.

David heads toward the back of the lot, jingling keys in his hand, backpack slung low by both straps on one arm, as though he's about to toss it into his car, a car maybe just a couple of strides ahead. "You got to have a plan, to know what kind of car you're looking for. If someone sees me, they have to think, 'Well he's just getting out to his car, that's all.' That's how I got to look. Like I'm going somewhere. I can't be looking into each car like some rip-off kid. So I decide—foreign cars, new cars, maybe American cars if they're big. And then I have to do a quick scope—What's in there? Are the doors locked? Could there be an alarm? So I pick a car at the back of the lot, and I walk there, make a noise with my keys, and maybe I'll peek in at two or three cars on the way. If they look good, I'll tap the door. If there's no alarm, I'll try the door. If the door opens, I'll grab whatever looks good on the floor. Drop it in the bag. Open the glove box, grab what looks good, shut it. If one car takes more than two seconds, it's no good. I got it down to like three, four body moves. That's it."

So David spends his lunch today walking in a pool of parking-lot glare. He fills his bag with small things. A miniature umbrella. A small metal flashlight. Lots of change. About thirty-five dollars from a wallet in an old Ford. ("Never take the wallet. Just the cash. Don't take anything with a name on it. Don't take anything that you can't say is yours. Like that make-up box, I'd like that for a girl I know, maybe give her a present. Or give it to my Mom. But if I get popped, I can't say it's mine, so I won't take it. And you got to memorize everything you put in your bag. You got to know it, so if they quiz you, you can be like you know what you took with you in your bag that morning.") He takes a book, *Jurassic Park*, from the last car in one row, and he keeps on walking, out of the lot, across the busy street, a few blocks down, and soon he's on a bus back to Lynn. He'll stop at the school near the end of the day to see his friends and spend some of his new money.

"Once I got stopped when I did the cars. Not where I was today," he says, "but not too far from there. Different town, though, so different cops. I don't want to be popped by the same cops twice, 'cause then they're gonna work harder to really get some evidence on me. So they grabbed me, they say 'What are you doing here, son?' I say, 'Nothing, just walking home.' 'Where do you live?' 'Lynn.' See, some things you can lie about, other things you can just be kind of general, or almost tell the truth. Where you live is the wrong thing to really bullshit on, because maybe the cops know where you say you live better than you do. So I said I live in Lynn. They said, 'You sure got a long walk home. Maybe you want a ride.' I say no thanks, I'm gonna take a bus. They say, come on over here, they take my bag, check my pockets, sit me in the back seat. I was cool, though, I didn't do a thing. I just sat there. Just quiet. They went through my stuff, but I didn't have anything, really. Man, maybe some money, some tapes. That's usually what you can get, then you can sell them to people you know for like a dollar or two. They shook out my backpack onto the lot. They tried to scare me—stick their faces in my face, say 'Watch yourself, brother,' like I'm their fucking brother—and then they told me to go and not come back. I thought maybe if I tried to pick up the stuff from the floor, it'd look more like it was my stuff, but they didn't like that, one walked right over, almost stepped on my hand and said really quiet, 'Get the fuck out of here. Now's your chance.' So I left, thought maybe they'd follow me till I was somewhere no one else could see me and then they'd pick me up again, but they just stayed there in their car in the parking lot. That was it. I was scared, yeah, but it was over and I still got home before dark."

Ask David about his family, and he talks about his mother. He loves his mother. She spends most of her days visiting relatives around Lynn, especially if someone is sick. In that case, she'll do a little cooking, a little shopping, to ease the burden a bit. If all in the family are well—and this is unusual; it's a big family—she'll go to church in the morning and linger, then visit one of her sisters for lunch and stay till three or four, when she goes back home to keep an eye on David, even though he's seldom there for long. But she wants him to check in after school, at least, and tell her where he's going. She likes to start cooking dinner then, but she knows she can't count on David to join her for the meal most nights, so an afternoon of cooking is a rare treat for her these days. She might chat on the phone instead, perhaps arguing with the cousins who still go to Mount Olive Baptist Church, the older, integrated Baptist Church in Lynn. David's mother goes to Mount Zion now instead. They've got a new pastor, an activist preacher who counsels discontent with the old white power structure in town. She likes him. David doesn't. He's embarrassed by what he considers the Reverend's complaining. He'd rather not be noticed himself, and even though he doesn't go to church, he says that if he *did* go to church, he would only go to hear a preacher who encouraged a quieter kind of godliness. Foot-stomping Mount Zion, tucked around the corner from English High, just past a boarded-up supermarket, turns him off.

David can talk about his mother for hours. Not only does he appreciate her concern for him, he also finds her amusing. "Always running around to this house and that house. She's everywhere all the time, her little shiny black pocketbook flapping away while she just runs down the block to Auntie's house. She's a funny lady." His father he won't talk about at all. Either he doesn't know much, or what he knows he chooses not to tell.

The Reverend at Mount Zion Baptist Church, David's mother's church, presides over a small white clapboard chapel. It was recently built after he managed to wring $250,000 out of a congregation of 250 mostly poor, mostly black men and women. He struggles to attract the young men like David who can go either way—toward stability and community, or toward crime. "We are fighting for our manhood here, every day," he says, and he means the manhood of these young men particularly. He wants to give them the feeling that coming into his church is an act of strength.

The funeral for the student killed on Valentine's Day at Central High was held at Mount Zion, and the Reverend began his service by asking the 200 students who sat among the hundreds of other mourners in the small church to call out with him, "I am somebody!," the line Jesse Jackson began chanting with students when he was a Chicago minister in the 1970s. Then the students walked, some alone, some alongside a friend, toward the silver coffin. Pauline Leslie, the girlfriend of the murdered student and the mother of his three-month-old baby daughter, fell to the floor in tears as she looked into the casket, and was helped out of the church by friends. She ran back in, screaming, and was surrounded by friends and family a second time and guided slowly out of the building. The stepfather of the murdered student also collapsed, overwhelmed by the sight of his stepson's body, and was taken by ambulance to a nearby hospital. After the funeral ended and most of the mourners had gone, a handful of students remained. One by one, they reached out and touched the murdered boy's hands.

Many students at English skipped school to be at the funeral, and more than one teacher at English did too. "I felt I had to come," said a woman who teaches history. "This isn't the first killing I've heard of in the years I've been teaching here, but— I don't know, it hit me harder than the others. I guess because it was at the school, and because he was so young. I think I also felt I should come because I saw how this hit my students so hard. Sometimes you teach these kids and they sit there staring at you for forty minutes, the bell rings and they leave, then the next roomful come in and *they* sit there, and on and on it goes like that, and you wonder sometimes what these kids really feel, what they really think.

"But I saw such grief. And Lord, today, here, the power of what they were feeling, it's almost unspeakable. In a way it's good to see this, and I don't mean this is not such a terrible thing—God, it is. But that the other students could be shocked by it is good. They feel it. They aren't used to it. That's very, very good. Good that they can still feel torn up by this terrible thing. They still see that this—excuse me—" She takes a breath and calms herself, and then continues: "That they still see the value of this life, and how horrible it is that this boy is dead, I think that's important. It's reassuring to me, as their teacher, as someone who goes in every day to live and work with these young people, to know they feel all this, that they can still be moved by it."

One of the vice-principals at English was an economics teacher there in the early 1960s, when Bill Murphy was a student. One day, he had to go to a funeral and arranged for a substitute. Looking back on it now, after almost twenty-five years of being a teacher, Murphy recalls that the substitute "just couldn't handle the class. She wasn't good at her job." Young Murphy had an exam coming up at the end of the day in another class, and he cut out to go study near his locker. The next day, seeing that he had been marked absent, the teacher asked Murphy where he'd been. Murphy said "I don't want to say, because you're not going to believe me."

"Of course I'll believe you, if you tell me the truth."

"I was in my locker studying, because this lady substitute couldn't teach."

"You expect me to believe that?" And then he suspended Murphy for cutting and for lying.

After lunch, Joe Patuleia catches up with the economics-teacher-turned-vice-principal on a couple of more recent suspensions, and then he hurries back to his own office to meet a teacher who has been waiting nervously for an "observation conference." The day before, Patuleia spent a period in her classroom, watching her teach. Today, she learns what he thought of her teaching, which he'll write up later as a formal part of her personnel file. She teaches math, the same subject that Patuleia taught at a middle-class suburban school for seventeen years before moving into administration. "Well," he says, settling into one of the two chairs in front of his desk, knee to knee with the teacher, "the first thing I have to say is that you showed great patience with that class," a ninth-grade business math class. "Especially that Joseph Wood," the teacher says. "He's already failed. He knows that. He's out of school for so long and then he's back in, acting so uncivilized." She fidgets, wrings her hands in her lap. A small woman, when she speaks, she seems even smaller—every word is tentative, every gesture self-conscious. She opens her black canvas book bag, looks through some papers—perhaps something she wants to show him—then shuts it and looks back up to Patuleia expectantly. Patuleia says, "If you can work with the good kids more closely, get them bonded, feeling that something important is happening in your class, then the outsider, when he comes back, he'll feel unwelcome, he won't get the same kick from being there giving you a hard time." She looks back blankly for a moment, and then nods her head vigorously. "Yes, yes," she says. "I actually like some of the kids." "When I taught this kind of class," Patuleia continues, "at this basic level, I tried to stay in motion, to circle around and look at the work they did at their seats, catch them doing things right. I'd put my hand on their shoulders, ask 'How you doing? Can you do that problem?' It shows that I care. 'You need some help with that?' That kind of thing. Staying in motion, keeping the contact close, keeping my presence close to each of them. That always helped a lot, made it feel that something real was going on for each of them." He goes over a form that he filled out while he observed her, and finds things to praise: "You were right there at the start of class checking the homework, that's important. And you communicated very clearly where each problem was in the book.

You gave them all a chance to know exactly where the work was coming from, where to find the problems. You had a good sense of where you were at the beginning and the middle and the end of the class. There was definitely a clear lesson happening." She smiles, nods again. "Yes," she says, "Yes, I've always thought: a beginning, a middle, an end. A lesson."

"You could have a faster pace in the class though," Patuleia then offers, "Move around a little more, give out more sheets. If you have each student working on more tasks in the outset of each class, you have more time to praise each individual student, and more of a chance for each kid to do something right that you can praise." "Yes," she says, "I do try to do that, to give them more tasks. I think that's important." "And you could ask them, once in a while, what are some of the things *you* want to learn, you know?" She doesn't seem to know. "If they're out there working after school, making change at a cash register, you can teach some shorthand for change-making. If any of them have kids, things like proportional pricing for baby formula—three ounces of this for a dollar versus five ounces of that for a dollar twenty-five. That kind of thing." "Oh yes," she says, looking relieved. "They work, they all work. Out there at the mall, or at Burger King. Sometimes I see one boy with his uniform in his bookbag—he won't wear it at school, he puts half what he makes into the other clothes he wears, I'm sure, expensive clothes I have no doubt—and the girls have children, I think two or three of them do, and I bet they have to do that, shop for this, shop for that."

As she leaves, Patuleia takes a deep breath. She taught for years in a junior high school in Lynn, and built up enough seniority to have her pick of new job openings. It is easier to picture her with younger students—eleven, twelve, thirteen year-olds-than with the challenging young men and women at English High. "She's got to dread that class," Patuleia says. "Really dread it. I wonder how she feels Sunday night, getting ready to jump back in the next morning." Later in the day, Patuleia meets with the math department chairwoman, and says to her more than once, "I don't think that our math department is a strong department. That's got to change."

Before the day is over, Patuleia sees the timid math teacher one more time, in a photograph. The yearbook salesman has come for a visit, bearing proof copies of all the photos for the seniors' souvenir volume. Month-old snow still covers much of the wide ring of open ground around the building, but for the yearbooks to be ready in June, they've got to start coming together now. The teachers look good in their photos; almost every one manages a look of dignity. Only the students' faces, most of them at least, betray the disbelief that they will indeed be graduating, that their snowy January poses somehow promise diplomas in the spring. Patuleia's experience reveals itself at times like this. The salesman is all smiles and handshakes, and gushes over the quality of the photos and all the good-looking faces. Patuleia bends over his desk looking through the stack slowly as the salesman awaits a final approval to go ahead and print the books. Then Patuleia looks up and asks, "Have these all been checked for fingers and signs and moons?" Fingers and signs and moons. "This is one thing that you only learn by the worst experience," Patuleia explains later. "You get a phone call from someone's grandmother who saw a kid flipping the bird on page thirty-three of the yearbook, or someone makes a gang sign, or your favorite student comes into your office with his copy of the book and says 'Did you see it?' And there it is, in one of those shots of kids playing ball outside the building, in a corner of the picture there's some kid's naked backside pressed against a classroom window."

In fact, gang signs almost never appear in yearbook photos at English High, or much of anywhere else around school. Some home-grown gangs mark out their territories around town, but they're all local tough guys. The larger, national gangs—the groups mostly out of L.A. with tentacles in Central and South American drug-producing regions—haven't yet made it to Lynn. Further north, though, in the old river-mill towns like Lawrence and Lowell, things are different. Dominican and Colombian gangs with links to drug networks in New Haven and New York City have begun to dominate the local business and family networks that lead new immigrants north to the U.S. and find them jobs—these days often illegal jobs, often connected to *Las Drogas*, the Anglo taste for cocaine and marijuana and heroin.

Alonso has seen the drug activity in the towns further north, and he appreciates the relative innocence of Lynn. Alonso is on his way to being a Dominican-American success story. He began in Miss Turner's Career English 9 class speaking little English, but he worked his way through it. Now, he's in a college-bound English class for juniors, and he's in Bill Murphy's honors American History class. He doesn't do well in science, but he doesn't expect to.

Alonso's mother works at a hospital as a cleaning woman, and his father is chef in a restaurant—good enough jobs in Alonso's eyes, though he has greater aspirations for himself. For the moment, though, he earns enough to run his car—a nice car, a five-year-old Ford Mustang—and to keep change in his pockets by "making deliveries."

"I won't do no crimes, I won't rob, I won't be violent," he says. "Never. I have a steady path. That's my vision: a steady path. I won't go off that path. I want something for myself that's a little bit more than what my family has now. I want to come home without dirt or food or garbage on my clothes. I want to live by my words and my brains. I don't want to have to live by my body. I think maybe I would be a social worker. To work with people, in their lives, but not so they pay me to do their dirty work, or cook their food, but that I have a profession. A way to dress nicely every day, to earn some kind of respect for who I am. I got to keep my steady path to make this happen, though, I know. I stay away from the fights, away from the *cliquas*, the guys who hang together for trouble. No. I learned some better lessons from my family. I learned from the school, too. I got something from them. I'm gonna be something more because I kept on the straight path, I did the work they asked me to do, I spent so much time reading through everything they gave me, every little page they said for homework, I came home, I read it again and again, and I learned something from that. So I got something to feel like it's my hope for a future off the street, with some respect. I see my mother or my father or my brothers, walking down the street, there are people who walk by, even if they don't know them, my family says 'Excuse me sir,' gets out of their way, they look like they're important people. That's what I want for myself.

"My brothers fix cars. They didn't finish school, but they work hard. They feel good, they have jobs, they have money, but they're just doing what my father did, really, except even dirtier, even harder work. I got something else. I really got something good. My plan, my path."

For now, working as a courier, Alonso spends about three hours on Saturdays and about three hours during the week—sometimes on Monday, sometimes on Tuesday—driving packages of drugs from Lowell to Chelsea. He doesn't know exactly what is in the packages—maybe heroin or cocaine. The not knowing is also part of his plan. "I don't get involved in the drugs. I don't want to see them. I wouldn't do that. I do the clean work, and I can do it because I'm respectable, I speak good English, I keep a clean car. People know I've got a goal, they would speak up for me if I had a problem. So I can do only the best part of this work and make enough money to keep going to school and keep a better thing ahead for me." He drives up to a distant cousin's apartment in Lowell, has a meal with him and his wife and their two small children, and on his way out, his cousin hands him a package about the size of a hard-cover book. It's all very social, and Alonso enjoys it; he feels important, respected. He drives down to Chelsea without stopping in Lynn, which is on the way. "Never stop," he says with great seriousness. "If you have a job to do, you do it first, don't think what time it is or where are your friends or you should go home for a rest first. Be reliable. That's why I can do what I do: I have the right attitude. That's why I'm going to get to be something better."

He goes to the third-floor apartment of a woman he doesn't really know. He sees her twice a week, but they don't talk; he just gives her the package and she says thank you and that's all. And then he goes back home. Sometimes he stops for a cup of coffee at a restaurant on the way. "I like that, to have coffee in a nice place. Maybe dinner will cost you twenty-five dollars, but coffee is just one dollar, two dollars. I always leave a nice tip, at least a dollar, sometimes two dollars, so they know I'm respecting them." Alonso doesn't have many friends, but this is by design. "Friends bring you down," he says. "They learn your secrets, they ask you for help you don't want to give them, they push you down the wrong path. For now, I can live with my own needs. When my goal is arrived, then I can think about how to have a friend."

Alonso's father suspects that his son is involved in the drug trade. They never speak about it, but he sees that his son has money to spend, he sees that he makes regular trips up to Lowell, and Alonso would not be the first decent young man in the family to work the drug trade—there are cousins, nephews. In fact, Alonso's father thinks his son is making a reasonable choice. "Do you think he should be like me, be a cook for his life? Or like his brothers? Working in dirt all day? You know what his brothers do? They take the drugs—they smoke, they sniff. Alonso doesn't do this. He uses the drugs to make something better for himself, not to drag himself down like his brothers. It's not a good thing, O.K., but the choice he makes now is not between good things."

Alonso doesn't go to church, and this, far more than his work in the drug trade, disappoints his father. "I don't go because I can't make confession," Alonso explains. "I can't make the sacrament. Maybe in a couple of years I can do that, but not yet."

Joe Patuleia's relations with the Hispanic students at English High are neither better nor worse than his relations with the other students. But he feels the missed opportunities that come from the limitations of his staff—particularly the fact that so few speak Spanish—and the cultural differences that he senses in the Hispanic families who send their children to his school. He explains: "The Hispanic families, most of them have a European mentality about schools." This sounds odd—most of the Hispanic families are not European; they're from Central and South America. He goes on: "They expect that the school will do its job without them coming down and second-guessing the teachers. They encourage their kids to follow the rules, without really understanding what the rules are all the time." His explanation risks sounding bigoted, but eventually his meaning becomes clear: the school has been given a trust by these families that it *should* merit, but, in truth, does not. He's not criticizing the Hispanic parents. He's criticizing the school for not deserving the trust they invest in it. "They expect their kids to do their job, which means go to school, pay attention, be obedient. But they expect us to do our job too; they see teachers as professionals, as part of an educated class that many of them aren't really part of. They see us as the experts in a way that most American-born parents don't. They give us so much trust. They don't come to Parents' Night just like I wouldn't come to Doctors' Night at the hospital. They trust us to do it right, and it simply takes a few years for the new immigrant families to adjust to life here, to begin to see that, maybe, we aren't going to do for their kids what they assume—because we're the teachers, because we're the ones with the authority—that will make their kids into American success stories. I'd like to become worthy of the trust they give us, but I'd settle for the unfortunate second-best choice, that they figure out how much we need their help, and they come to more meetings, they check up on their kids more, and on their kids' teachers."

Alonso represents a new kind of criminal in Lynn. He is, above all, nice. His teachers, his neighbors, and even the police see him as a good kid because he works hard to do everything they want him to do. His bad acts are in addition to, not instead of, his good ones. Old-time Lynners have little experience with this kind of trouble—polite, respectful, conformist trouble. They are more used to the dangerous young men who curse and rave, who drop out of school and pave early-morning bus stops with the broken glass of their late-night binges. And Lynn does still have its share of these young men and women, mostly the children of the white working class lured to town two or three generations ago to work in the General Electric plants, the tanneries, and the shoe factories.

Early in the nineteenth century, Lynn had become a national center for shoemaking; the industry rested on the collective skills of thousands of artisans who each made about sixty shoes a day, mostly by hand. The Lynn Lasters Union was a powerful labor confederation, and had a national impact, fostering some of the earliest strains of American labor socialism. Then, in the 1880s, a black man living in a segregated rooming house in Lynn invented the hand-method lasting machine, which effectively automated the shoe industry.

With the machine, a single skilled operator could produce not sixty but six hundred shoes a day. But the union fought the machine bitterly, injecting race into their struggle by naming the hand-method lasting machine "the nigger machine." After years of bitter conflict, the matter was settled by fire. In 1889, eighty acres of wooden factories and workers' homes burned to the ground. The following year, there was little work to be had for shoemakers in Lynn, and many of the union members migrated down to Whitman, south of Boston, and to other shoemaking towns in New England. As the factories in Lynn rebuilt, all installed the machines, and eventually they supported less than half the jobs that shoemaking men worked in Lynn in 1889, a foretaste of the workingman's fate in Lynn for the next century.

Today, with the shoe-making industry clustered in South America and Asia, and with General Electric whittling away at its workforce year by year—sometimes even month by month—the blue-collar economy of Lynn is all but gone, and the sons and daughters of the old industrial working class haunt the town. Brought up in the 1950s and 1960s to believe that hard work and physical strength would be enough to secure a lifetime's work, today many Lynners in their forties and fifties are unemployed, and many more live lives constrained by the hourly wages of security guards, waitresses, and retail clerks. Of *their* children, the first generation to know from the start that the old wage-economy would offer them nothing, some succeed at school and prosper. Then they leave. Others drop out and find few paths before them. They stay.

June is determined not to be one of those who stay. She liked school enough to push herself through, and now and then she found a teacher who really cared for her. Ken Curtis, the former vice-principal, was one of them. Another is Mr. McManus, a vocational math teacher. In his record-keeping class, June feels special. "I'm one of his finest students," she says, enjoying the sound of that phrase. "He really likes me, and when I start to skip too often, when I'm in trouble, he says 'June, c'mon, get on the ball, take care of yourself.' My mother won't do that for me, reach out for me to help me like that, so I've got Mr. McManus, and at least I've got something." She lives with her mother and her two sisters, but uncomfortably. "My mother cares, I know she does, but she just steps back when I have trouble. I'm the middle child, she says, the rebel. From how she sees it, that means there's nothing else she can do for me when I have a problem.

"I've had a lot of problems, a lot of them from my family. I've tried to figure out how to deal with everything sometimes, how to keep myself together better. Last year, I was thinking that maybe if I knew who my father was, I'd be less depressed. My mother was married to a guy named Ziggy, and around that time he died. I thought that would be the right time to talk to her. Well, I found out that this guy's brother—Ziggy's brother—was my biological father. I have a hard time understanding how my mother got into these relationships with Ziggy, first of all, and then with my biological father, who she's seeing again now. Actually she's living with him now. But I'm glad she told me. It explains some things, I think. About me, I mean. For example, you know, I've always looked for the father-figure." She pauses, thinking about this fact. "Most of my friends are guys."

One of these guys is Johnny. Johnny was, briefly, a student at English High, but he dropped out after a few weeks, joined an alternative school program at a public job-training center, and eventually left school altogether a few months ago, at fifteen. For all those Lynners who fear young black men in town, Johnny is a reminder that young white men can merit the same fear.

June met him at Flax Pond, one of the murky still pools in Lynn Woods Reservation. "I was in love with a kid named Alan— oh, he's so beautiful, I still think about him. After a few days hanging out with him, though, I got to know him, and I was finally like, 'He's a dink. Beautiful looking, but a dink.' I figured him out and I didn't want to see him anymore. But I was still going to the Pond to watch the guys all play basketball, and one of his friends there was Johnny. He was real nice to me. When he saw me, he'd come over and say 'How you doing,' and all that, though this is when these guys were trying to be real hard, so it was more like 'Whassup.' They were all part of The Crew, which was like a gang, but really they were just a bunch of kids, nothing bad. Johnny stole cars, that was the worst of it then. This is maybe two years ago, my first year at English."

They dated seriously for a few months, but then June began to pull back. "I really cared about Johnny, but I saw how all these guys he hung out with were starting to carry knives and stuff. I just felt like, 'I'm sick of this.' Then once in a while someone would pull out a gun and I'd be like, 'Put that thing away!'

"I just walked away from it. Johnny wound up getting arrested for stealing cars. They sent him to Youth Services. He'd send me letters, but the more trouble all these guys had, the less I wanted to be part of it. So I stopped seeing him for a while.

"My little brother loved Johnny. He was sad when Johnny stopped coming around, when he was locked up or when I told Johnny I didn't want to see him anymore. Me and Johnny would play the Mommy and Daddy role babysitting my brother. It felt good. You know, comfortable. But it just was too much sometimes, the way they would act hard, showing off their guns."

June broke up with Johnny, but he called and wrote her notes, and soon they were back together. It became a pattern: every so often June would tell Johnny she didn't want to see him anymore because of all the risks he took and the violence in his life, but after a few days she'd welcome his overtures and they'd pick up where they'd left off. Then in the fall, they went through their longest separation, first weeks and then months.

While they were apart, Johnny was stabbed at a party by group who called themselves the Tower Hill Kids, after a hill in the Lynn Woods Reservation crowned with an old stone lookout tower. Johnny was seriously wounded, taking deep cuts in his back and legs.

While he was in the hospital recovering, June called him. "I heard about the stabbing about a week before Valentine's Day. I called him at the hospital, then I went to see him, and when I was leaving, he said 'Could I kiss you goodbye?' and I said yes. He hugged me, and he asked me if I would come back the next day. I said sure. Then before I went back I was thinking about whether I would want to date him again, and I thought, 'He's treating me nice. Yeah, I'll do it.' Then when he was out of the hospital, he couldn't leave his house—he was still hurt. So I helped out, went to the store for him, picked up things, cooked for him sometimes. I liked it."

June spent a lot of time with Johnny while he was convalescing, and she also spent a lot of time with Johnny's friends who came around to keep him company. One was a boy named Dale, whom June had once dated. "Dale doesn't have parents," she explains. "He's had a lot of foster families, and he never really had anyone to love him. He needed that, but I wasn't the right one. I didn't have enough power to help him." June says that it was Dale who brought guns into The Crew. He was also the first to spend time in an adult prison. "They all came over to my house one night, but I wasn't there. I was coming home late that night because I stopped at the store to pick up a couple of things, and when I got home my mother's boyfriend said they had just left—I missed them by a couple of minutes only. So they went off to a park. Dale started joking around, shooting his gun into the air. Some of the other guys with him told him to stop it, to give up the gun, you know, hand it over. But some other gang heard the shots and came over and yelled something and then they were all fighting.

"Then, for some reason, some guy drives up and tells everybody to stop fighting. Just some guy who was driving by. Dale pulls out his gun, points it at this guy and says 'You don't want to be here.' But the guy doesn't blink, you know, he just keeps talking at them. So Dale shoots out his windshield. Then the cops came, they arrested Dale and put him away for a while.

"Isn't it funny, that if I just hadn't gone to the store, if I was home at the regular time instead of a little later, maybe Dale wouldn't have been put in jail? But it was good for him. You know how they say jail can be good for some people? For him, it was true. He was too intense. He needed to be in jail for a while."

Another visitor at Johnny's house while he healed was a boy named Freddie. Freddie lived with his stepbrother and made a living selling cocaine. June never liked Freddie, though she didn't really know him well. "The one time he was at my house was when I was having money problems, and I told this one kid in the group I wished I could have a nice meal, and he said, 'C'mon, let's go to your house, I'll get a steak and cook you up a nice steak dinner.' So he came and it was great, but Freddie came along with him, and he just had a high opinion of himself, you could tell. He thought he was all that. I didn't care for him at all."

Another day, while Johnny was still staying at home, June drove Dale and Freddie and a couple of others to a Wendy's for some food. Johnny heard about it and got angry. "Johnny was pretty stupid about it. I had no strong feeling for any of those guys, except a strong feeling that I thought Freddie was a jerk. So I wasn't happy when Johnny got so worked up about me driving them to Wendy's." June had just gotten her car, a

'78 Chevy Nova, and she would drive anybody anywhere. She just liked driving. But she didn't like Johnny's jealousy.

Soon, Johnny was strong enough to start going out of his house again. His injuries kept him from stealing cars for a while, though, and June took to driving him around. One afternoon, June was driving through Salem with Johnny and a friend of his in the car. They were on Bridge Street, a road that winds around the working port area of Salem's shoreline, right along the Parker Brothers Game Company headquarters and assembly plant. The roads were icy and a woman pulling out of a side road hit June's Chevy broadside. "I'm lucky I was in that car. It's a big car, and it can take that kind of damage, but some other cars can't."

The woman got out of her car and started yelling at June. "She was screaming 'You stupid teenagers!' and shit like that. But it was really her fault. I saw her coming, but I could see that she didn't see us. Her head was turned the wrong way; I could tell that she was just going into the road without seeing. I knew if I braked I would skid on the ice, so I honked and tried to swerve out of her way, but it didn't matter. She just went right into us. So she's there yelling, making a scene, and we call the cops. She tells the cop we were drinking and we threw a bottle into the woods near the road. He looks around, finds an old bottle—you could tell it's been there for weeks—and he's smiling, he asks is this ours, we say no, and he throws it back into the woods.

"But the guys are getting nervous. Johnny's friend especially, he's worried. The cop at the window asks for all our names, and that's it, he just jumps from the car and runs like crazy, but he only gets a few steps. There's another cop there and he grabs him, slams him into the rear window. He had a warrant out on him, and they got him. I think he gave them a fake name, I think. Then the other cop swings around to Johnny and pulls him out of the car, all tough and hard. Johnny is like, 'I just got stabbed, take it easy, I'm chill.' That's what he was saying, 'I'm chill, I'm chill,' but the cop didn't care, he was slamming him against the car, hurting him. So then Johnny hit him.

"Now Johnny had a warrant out for him, too, for car theft, which was his usual thing. He just stole cars all the time, and all the time he got caught. He had no conscience, really. He just saw a car, thought 'Hey, that looks nice, I'd like a car like that,' and he'd just grab it, steal it and drive it around for a while. But he always got caught. At first, he wanted to. He thought it was cool to be in DYS, it was tough, with the cool kids, the hard kids.

"So that day he's got a warrant out for his real name, and he tells the cops his name is something else. They take him into the jail anyway, charge him with assaulting an officer. Later I go down to the station to get him. I say I'm his fiancée, can I please see him—the fake name? And they release him in my custody.

"This is the kind of shit I go through for Johnny. To be with him, I have to become a con artist."

While she was still thinking over this latest adventure with Johnny—thinking about whether or not to leave him for good—someone slipped June a note in the middle of Mr. McManus's record-keeping class. "It was third period. I get this note, it says 'I just want you to know that Johnny is my boyfriend now.' It's from some girl named Penney. I never even heard of her. I just left class—I had to leave class, this was like a major shock (and went to the bathroom. I punched the wall. My head was spinning, I mean, who was this girl?

"I go down to the telephones and call Johnny and I say 'Who's Penney?' And he says, 'Oops.' I said 'Oops? Oops? That's all you fucking say, Oops? Then fuck you!' And that was it, that was the end of us."

Later, June met Penney, and they became good friends. They met at Johnny's first court date, when he was formally charged with murdering his friend Freddie.

Chapter Four

Games

Angie knows who shot the two boys at Lynn Central High, but she won't tell. "The police've been coming around all the time, to my house, to school, taking me to the police station, making my life hard. They think I know who killed those boys, but I don't think it's my place to tell. It's just not my place."

Propriety means a lot to Angie. Being proper, trying to keep to her place, is how she keeps a clear boundary between her own life and the kind of life many of her friends live. "The girls I grew up with, most have babies now. They think when they leave high school, their life's going to get so much better, so they have a baby, they're not going to be lonely anymore, and they stay home. Then they see what it's really like, and they go crazy.

"What are you going to do if you're a young girl and you're in your mother's house all day long with a baby? Nobody comes by, nobody thinks you want them around, and you probably don't want them around anyway, because who do you know who can treat a baby the right way who you want to spend any time with for yourself? So they get a job at Star Market. I'm telling you, I have five, six girlfriends right now with babies at home who live their lives out of their house and just go out to work at Star Market. They just count the days going by. That's it for them.

"You should see these girls. They look older than my mother. Last year, I made a decision in my life. My grades weren't good, and I looked around and I saw what was happening to my girl-friends and I said no, no way, that's not going to be the story of my life. If I didn't move myself up, I'd just be another punk, with a baby, on welfare. I couldn't face that. And my mother wouldn't have it either. She told me straight: don't come home pregnant, because that's where I draw the line. You come home with some man's baby, and you are on your own."

Angie's mother is a social worker with the state welfare office in Salem, the next town over. She owns the home she lives in with Angie and her two younger sisters. It sits on a main road in Lynn, a road that starts near the ocean among the large older homes, and runs straight through town, winding up among derelict and half-burned structures at the edge of open parklands. Angie's house is about halfway down that road, not far from English High. It is a large home, three stories, an indistinct brown. Over the front door, a sign: No Trespassing.

"I want to be a doctor. *Will* I be a doctor? I don't know, but I'll be something. Something far from here. People tell me I should be a lawyer because I've got a big mouth. That's not going to be my way. I don't want to be just a talker, I want to know what I'm talking about, you understand? I want to be the one with the knowledge to move something forward, to make something happen. When people say to me, be a lawyer, I'm thinking they look at me and figure I'll be nothing more than I am right now. But I'm going to school to be more, to be something different. High school's not doing that for me yet, but college will.

"Too many of the kids I grew up with don't see that they're not finished yet. Girls wake up and say, 'Well, here I am, what can I do? Can't do nothing, really, so I'll just get used to that, maybe have a baby.' Boys say, 'Well, I'll just go out and make myself some money, 'cause that's all there is for me.' They don't see that maybe it's so today, but tomorrow there's a chance for something else. Like my last boyfriend, he's living a fat life. New car. Clothes. Gold. Goes out. With him, I went out all the time, dinner, movies, like we were really something, really people you could knock on our door and we say yes we live here, here we are, we're done *becoming*, we already *are*, we're already finished, like we're forty years old.

"He's a dealer, that's where his money is. You see some stupid black man wandering down the street high on crack, maybe my boyfriend has some of that man's money in his pocket, maybe he's buying me dinner with that money. But I'm not ready yet. I'm not ready for that. I'm trying to be something else."

Most of Angie's teachers like her, but some think she gets away with too much. "She's smart, yes, but too smart," says her English teacher. "Verbal skills, they say she's got. Well, she's got too much verbal skill, in my opinion, shooting her mouth off every day she's in here. I ask her where her work is, she's giving me a story about her sister's sick, the principal's taking her to a meeting, she's in on some black thing, whatever it is, whatever it is *that day*, she doesn't have two stinking pages of homework I give out. And that's *if* she's there. Since February—that's two months—she's missed ten classes. Ten classes! Do you think I'd be getting my paycheck if I missed ten classes? I'd be delighted to be out with meetings, out turning heads instead of in this dirty room teaching these kids every day, but I have some responsibilities, and she does too. So where is she? Today. Where is she today? She wasn't in my class today. And I want to know where the hell she is."

Some days when she's not in class, Angie is home watching television, or out, visiting friends who left school or graduated, seeing them and their babies. This day, though, Angie missed her English class even though she was in school. She spent that period in one of the vice-principal's offices, talking with him, and with a detective from the Lynn Police Department about the shootings at Classical High. The police say that they are talking to everyone, hundreds of interviews with hundreds of people. But Angie is getting special attention. She tells the police that she thinks the shooting was about a chain, a gold chain someone stole, but she says she's only heard that from some other students, she doesn't really know for sure herself, and she doesn't remember exactly which other students told her. She tells the police this several times over the next month, and eventually they come around to see her less. Then they name a suspect, Carl Hardaway, someone Angie's old boyfriend knew. The *Item* reported:

A 22-year-old Lynn man has been charged with the murder of a Classical High student who was gunned down near school grounds last month in front of more than a dozen students.

The murder warrant was issued for Carl Hardaway, 23 Hanover Circle, Apartment No.1. The apartment building is located near Classical High. On the day of the shooting, the suspect was last seen running in that general direction, police said.

An investigation that stalled due to lack of cooperation from frightened students who witnessed the February 14 shooting, finally came together this week.

At first, the police wouldn't speculate about Hardaway's motive. Grady says they don't have to: "It was the chain. I know it. Everybody who knows knows it. It was the chain. He stole a chain, so the other guy pulled him out and popped him. That's it. Over." Sandy says he knows, too: "Man, it was a sorry thing. But you know, it happens when you mess with people late at night. It was a thing at the Palace, that club in Saugus. He was out there, the kid who died, and he said something to this other kid's girl, and that was it. The other kid—now maybe I know who it was, maybe I don't—he wouldn't take it. So he got stupid. I know how he felt—you got to do something, you got to be *seen* to do something hard when you get embarrassed at night like that, in front of your crew, you know, they're looking at you, watching you, thinking 'Now what's this boy of ours made of,' you know? So he came through the next day, to show he was made of some hard stuff."

The police offer their own ideas. "We don't believe it had anything to do with the school," Lieutenant Robert Carter says later. "In fact, the boy who died didn't even make it to school that day. He was just hanging out *near* school. If he had went to school that day, he wouldn't have been shot. Not if he had been where he was supposed to be, in class at that time, instead of hanging out somewhere else.

"These are not bad schools. Yes, there are some bad kids who go there. But everybody's trying to make things work. If your kid is a *student* student, they'll probably do well. But if your kid is a mediocre type of student and more of a follower, he could get into a problem that's too much to handle.

"These schools still do function as high schools. It's there if the student can take hold of it. But there's plenty of opportunity for trouble, too." Enough opportunity that Carter, who lives in Lynn, chose to send his children to private schools. "In this one case at Classical High," Carter says, "we now know that the shooting was over a jacket. Some kids made fun of this one young man's jacket, and he felt they were making fun of him. So he went home and got a gun to straighten things out. And that's what he did. He straightened things out.

"Will he be caught? Yes, he will. No question. We will get him."

For Angie, it doesn't matter much whether he's caught or not. She's planning out her life for the next few years, and as she sees it, that life has little to do with Lynn and nothing at all to do with people who shoot each other over chains or girls or jackets. As the days have been warming a bit, her school plans have changed. She's thinking less about the big private universities in Boston and setting her sights instead on a biology program at North Adams State College, a program geared toward minority premed students. "It's far away, but not too far," she says. North Adams is about one hundred and fifty miles from Lynn, in the Berkshire Hills. It's dairy farming country, though the culture—tourism trade is big as well—classical music at Tanglewood, modern dance at Jacob's Pillow, and theater at a Edith Wharton's old summer home, The Mount, are all near, and all draw moneyed guests from New York City. The change for Angie will be dramatic.

Back at English High, spring has been approaching with perhaps less grace than it carries with itself in the Berkshires, but the charms of bright sun and warming winds are substantial nevertheless. Lunchtimes have been stretching. Though the same forty-minute period presents itself inside school, more and more students—especially seniors, who become more confident with each passing day that they will indeed graduate, that one more absence couldn't really stop them at this point—leave the building as lunch begins. They return an hour or two later, if at all.

The melted snow has revealed a scrubby green lawn around the school building, budding with scraps of waste—candy wrappers, discarded loose-leaf paper, greasy paper plates coated by the remains of pizza—that clash with the hopeful blooms of delicate fruit trees and trestle-climbing plants along many of the simple wooden homes surrounding the school.

Inside the building, wintry fears still have their place. I'd been watching an art teacher for a few weeks, noticing how well he turns his students toward the subtleties of printmaking and painting. Peeking though his window, I often see a dozen or so students loom over this small man. Anywhere else, I'd think they were about to pounce on him, steal his money and his leather shoes. But here they look over his shoulder at whatever hidden object he holds, and they listen for long minutes, totally focused on the ideas this man is offering them.

I asked Bill Murphy who on the teaching staff he respected most, and he pointed to the art teacher. "He does a great job, without any flash. The students really take to him." So I asked him one day if I could visit his class and watch him teach. "Is this an order?" he asked. "No, no," I said, "I've just heard good things about you and I wanted to just sit in the back of your room and watch you teach a little." "Well," he said, turning away, "if the principal orders me to, I'll have to say yes." "I'm sorry," I said, embarrassed to have made him so uncomfortable, "I was just asking. No one's ordering anyone to do anything." "Oh really? Well, that's not how things work here."

A few weeks later, I saw the art teacher again, while I was trailing Joe Patuleia for a day. Patuleia knocked on his door during a class, and called him into the hall. Patuleia had a drawing of the school building in his hand that an art student had made. He was planning to use it for a brochure about Lynn English High. "If you could just ask him to make this stand out a little more," Patuleia was saying, "and make these letters bigger, maybe move them over here." The art teacher took the sheet from Patuleia, said, "Yes, yes, uh-huh," sighed loudly, and then said "Well, I'll just do it. I'll fix it for you." Patuleia said, "Maybe the kid would? I mean, he might like to." "No, no, it's fine. I'll do it. I'll have it tomorrow." Then he turned and went back to his class.

"Some of them are still afraid," Patuleia said as we headed down the hall. "More time. That's what we need, more time together. They'll figure it out, we'll all be a little less nervous."

Today, Angie and her friend June have decided to work on their own nerves by taking the afternoon off. Long past the end of lunch period, they sit in a cheap diner about a mile from the school, drinking coffee, not seeming young at all. "I like June," Angie says, "because she sees deeper meanings in things." As they sit there drinking their coffee, Angie holds up her coffee cup. It's handmade—that's why she likes this diner especially, they serve coffee in cups that look identical, but really aren't. All are a standard shade of diner-blue, but they feel heavier than most commercial coffee mugs, and it's true that if you look closely, you can see the slight ripples and rings of the potter's hand. "I love this," June says. "I can hold this cup and I know that my hand is where her hand was—the person who made this. It's like, she made it for me, so I could drink from her cup and think about her. It's more than I can say of most people—that they would do something to bring me anything important. But this cup means that there was someone who did, someone who could reach me."

"I love that," Angie says, smiling at her friend. Later, she says, "June can see things like that. You wouldn't expect it from her; she hangs out with some scary people. But she's better than they are, I can say that flat out. She's a better person."

Early in April, June takes a trip to Connecticut to visit her older sister, who works as an au pair for a family there while going to college part-time. The day after she gets back, someone tells her that Freddie has been missing for a few days. "It didn't bother me, because I didn't like him anyway. I figured the dude's probably off wandering, no reason for anybody to be worried, really." But Freddie's brother *is* worried, perhaps because he knows Freddie is involved in the drug trade, and that many people have reasons to wish him harm.

On Monday, April 18, a front-page story in the *Lynn Item* takes June by surprise. The headline: "Body Found in Lynn Woods."

Three boys who were in Lynn Woods to watch a mountain bike race Sunday afternoon discovered the body of an 18-year-old man lying face down about 200 yards off a heavily-used trail.

The body was Freddie's.

Two days later, police name Johnny as the suspect in Freddie's killing, and issue a warrant for his arrest. They say that Freddie left his house one evening not long ago, went to see a friend, and then went out to Lynn Woods to meet Johnnie. Then, Johnnie killed him.

Lynn Woods was once a refuge from the busy industry of Lynn's shoe factories, a place for a quiet walk under old trees. Even earlier, as a patch of open land near the shore with the highest elevation for miles, it sprouted stone lookout towers. British ships could be seen miles offshore during the Revolution and the War of 1812; whalers and trading ships could be

seen far enough out that by the time they docked all the whalers' wives and all the traders' agents would line the wharf, pray-
ing thanks for safe-returning men, or counting contracts in
their heads.

More recently, though, the thickets of Lynn Woods have
drawn their share of horror. A generation ago, the Woods were
still a kind of refuge, where kids could go for adventure, or
lovers for solitude. (Bill Murphy lost a tooth there in 1963,
when he was a sophomore at English High and had just had
braces unwired from his mouth. His bike turned over and he
slammed his jaw onto a rock. His tooth popped right out. He
put it in his pocket and the next day a dentist in Boston wired
it back in.)

Today, though Lynn Woods can still draw families for noon
cookouts, at night the place is fearsome. Every so often, bodies turn up there.

The picture of Johnny in the newspaper offers a strikingly
young-looking boy—his narrow eyes and the tilt of his head are
defiant, but his hair trails over his eye as a small boy's might,
and his soft features could belong to a twelve-year-old. He is
sixteen.

In the days that follow, the *Item* reports that Freddie was not
necessarily killed by the bullet wounds in his corpse; he had
also been bludgeoned, probably by a heavy rock. The corpse
is not as clean as investigators would like, though. Some wounds
are obscured by the ravagings of animals. The newspaper also
notes that Johnny threw a party about a week after Freddie
first went missing. June didn't go. "I just didn't want to see
Johnny, that's all. But I had no idea he killed him. I didn't
even know Freddie was dead. Nobody did. It was just a party.
You know, Johnny called Freddie's brother every day, seeing if
Freddie was back yet. He was worried like everybody else, or
at least that's how it looked then."

Lynn police announce that they've begun searches in several states. Johnny is thought to be on the road to Missouri,
where he has a friend. His mother, who is only thirty-three,
appears in the newspaper and on local television news shows,
saying that it was an accident, Johnny and Freddie were target-
shooting together and something just went wrong. She calls
for her son to turn himself in. She says they all loved Freddie—

she and Johnny and the others in The Crew—that he used to
come to their apartment, that she cooked for him all the time.
Johnny is certainly innocent, she says. He's run just because he
is scared. (June knew Johnny's mother well. "She'd been in jail
a lot. She was trying to win him back, to love him. She really
wanted him to respect her. But all he could remember was
how when he was a little boy, how she would hurt him. She'd
leave him in charge when he was five—she'd go out to bars, go
get high—he'd be in charge of his little brother. He hated it.")

On the 23rd of April, the police catch Johnny. The front
page of the *Item* shows a shaven-headed young man wearing a
black "Crew" T-shirt, held by a middle-aged, round-faced Lynn
police officer. Johnny had apparently gone to Missouri to hide
at the house of a friend from Lynn who'd moved west, but
he'd been scared off when police—locals and Lynn police together—turned up to search the house. (While they were out
there, the Lynn police took the opportunity to arrest Johnny's
friend on outstanding Lynn warrants.)

Later in the day, friends of Freddie break into the house
where Johnny was arrested and beat the three people there,
presumably in revenge for hiding Freddie's killer.

June was shocked to hear Johnny accused of Freddie's murder, but it made a certain amount of sense to her. "These kids
began real innocent. Sure, they'd carry knives, but only for
protection. They weren't looking to hurt anybody. Then one
guy started getting them all excited about having guns, and
then they wanted more money, some of them were dealing
crack and cocaine, and something bad was coming. You could
see it. It started real innocent—really, it started with just playing basketball at Flax Pond, but then it got to guns and that
was the end of being innocent."

When Johnny's new girlfriend Penney came to June's gradu-
ation party, they wound up talking all night. "Everyone else
went home or fell asleep, but we just sat there talking until six.
We talked about everything, including Johnny. At first we both
said Johnny didn't do it. Maybe it was one of the others. Maybe
the one with the guns. But they were both pretty fucked up—
they would go out at night and drink and do coke and they'd
be totally bagged, so you can't be sure what somebody could
do when they get like that.

"Johnny says another kid did it. I don't know anymore if that's true. Now it's like, there's some evidence that the police have that made them go after Johnny and not someone else. That's got to be something. Johnny says that nobody's going to find out the truth until he gets out of jail. He's got some plan, I guess. But that might be a long time from now. It's hard to really think about that, how long he might be in jail. Could be a long time."

Joe Patuleia reads about the killing of Freddie, but he does not know that the accused killer was once an English High student. And while he knows June and likes her, he has no idea of her involvement. Today, murder is far from his mind. Instead, he's thinking about money.

"This man," he is saying, "has put in his years here, but he's not earning his money today." The principal stands in the second-floor gym, watching the basketball coach run drills. The drills are loose and slow. Some of the players—Jay, most notably—run lay-ups with grace, rising and half spinning and letting the ball roll off their extended hands, up into the basket. But they are the exceptions. Others look too soon to their buddies watching under the backboard, distracted by self-consciousness, half-laughing as they rise up, blowing basket after basket. "At any given moment, half of the players are standing still. Why? How are they learning by standing still? One day this coach will retire. This guy's put in the years; I can't take him out now. And he's winning his games. But soon enough his time will end."

The day is warm. The same sun that drew lunch-hour students out of the building and away from school still lights up the early afternoon and slowly melts the last traces of old snow lacing the grass. Classes are still in session, but the basketball courts outside English High are actually busier than the courts indoors. The players out here lack the athleticism of the team players inside, but their energy is more obvious—they are here to have fun. They bark, yell, and squeal freely. Under one hoop a group of boys all call out to each other in Spanish and leap toward the ball each time it reaches a margin of their half-court. They shoot infrequently, passing again and again and again. Across from them, a group of girls plays, clearly for fun and not for competition. They shoot baskets, gather rebounds, but don't dribble much, and take the time to talk to each other about the boys walking by in low-hung jeans, wide tank-tops and unlaced sneakers. Two young men—maybe students, maybe not—buzz the nearby parking lot on a small motorbike without license plates.

There is a feeling of generosity outside the building that is rare inside. Among students, some kind of wariness is the rule inside English, but outside, with a bit of April sunshine, they shout out good feeling—"Good Shot!" "*Mi hombre!*" loud laughter—that the very fact of being *inside* school seems to preclude. Soon enough, the schoolday is over and more students pour out the school's back doors. The girls give up their court to a new group of boys.

"I don't really want to play basketball anyway," says Maria. "I'd rather watch those boys play." She laughs, and her friends laugh with her. One of the boys has heard, though, and looks over. "What you looking at?" she challenges, and he turns back to the bouncing ball. Why has she cut school to play ball right next door? "There's nothing for me in that school. I want to be a dancer. I *will* be a dancer. What I need from this place is to pass my classes so I can go and study at a real school when my years here are up, a real dance school. I will give them only as much as they make me have to give, but no more. It's a lousy school, really. The teachers aren't educated enough. They don't know how to teach. If they knew how to teach, we wouldn't be getting such low grades. They don't care if you do go in to class, anyway. They fail the students they don't like, pass the students they do like. If they see me less, that's better, so they won't know me well enough to decide they don't like me. They aren't really creative people, you know? I want something they can't give me, and what they have to offer, I don't want."

Nearby, another group of boys has taken up a baseball game. They don't have gloves, though, so it's a hitter's game—no one has the will to throw a runner out at first or second base for fear of breaking a teammate's hand. Just long fly balls, long tosses from the fielders toward the infield, and lots of fielders chasing baserunners around the basepaths. One of the ballplayers is Dominican, and he wants to become a professional baseball player. "It's the game of Dominica, man," he says, smiling. But if that doesn't happen, he'd like to be a policeman. "To be a cop is a good deal—you can be outside, have some security, get some respect. You can live a good life, have a house, have some time to spend with a family. I'm not looking to make a million dollars, you know?" He plays with energy, chasing down ball after ball hit out to left field. And he hits with tremendous power, twisting his face into a knot as his bat connects, pulling back hard on his shoulders at precisely the right moment and tracing low curves with his balls, just over the outstretched bare hands of the fielders who are happy enough to reach without grasping those hard-hit balls that drop, time after time, far enough out for home run after home run.

One boy walking out of school at the end of the day stands out in his ripped white T-shirt with slogans scrawled across the fabric, streaks of blue dye in his hair. This is Constantine. "The other kids," Bill Murphy tells me, "make his life miserable. They can't stand the fact that he's different. And he certainly is different. He wants to be an oddball, but with reason. One day, he walked around the school hanging up signs that said 'Question Authority.' No one else in this building would do it. That took character.

"Once, when he was walking into one of my classes, I heard some of the other kids make remarks. You couldn't miss it, they were open about their insults. I stopped them and said I admired Constantine—here's a guy who's really an individual, and isn't that what our country stands for? The chance to stand alone, to challenge the people around you? Let him dress differently, I said, that's the kind of challenge we need. They weren't really with me on that, so I said, 'You know, one day I'm gonna come in here wearing a dress, just to make a point.' And man, they went wild, they were just roaring with laughter. 'Well,' I said, 'the Romans ruled half the earth for fifteen hundred years wearing dresses.' But they really weren't tuning in to what I was saying. They just enjoyed giving Con a hard time."

Near the main entrance at English a small display case offers "English on Parade"—clippings from the local newspapers about the school. Most are the usual stories about top students and their college plans. A few feature faculty profiles. Others address crime: "Teens Tackle Violence," "Teens Stage Summit," "Lynn Teens Confront Violence." One article in particular stands out. It features a large picture of two girls standing beside a grandfather clock, one tall, blond, smiling; the other smaller, darker, with a mild expression. They seem to illustrate the two halves of English High—the old picture-book image of blond American youth beside the new, unfamiliar face of an immigrant girl. The headline reads "Heroes: Girls, Inc. to Honor English High Students." "Two seniors at English High," the article begins,

> have been named winners of the 1994 'Girl Hero' awards to be presented by Girls Incorporated of Lynn.
>
> Tham Net, a native of Cambodia, won the 'Girl Hero' award from Girls, Inc., and Kerry Jo Behn, the senior class president, will receive the Betty Dempsey Scholarship.
>
> Each girl will receive $500 towards her college education. Girls, Inc. will also name three winners of the 'She Knows Where She's Going' award.
>
> Net, 18, has a 4.32 grade-point average and is a member of the National Honor Society at English, which is an achievement for a girl who fled the Khmer Rouge with her family, spent several years in a refugee camp in Thailand, and came to the United States in 1987. She has been speaking English for barely seven years.

The visitor to English High is invited to reflect on these girls. One, the class president; the other, refugee. Now that they have been brought together at Lynn English High—both given awards and money, both invested with great hope—the prospect that each might become at least a little bit like the other is still astounding.

The next day, between classes, Joe Patuleia pulls Bill Murphy aside in the hallway for a quick talk. Before he begins, Patuleia smiles awkwardly to a science teacher pushing a shopping cart through the halls. The science teacher has been in the building eight years, but still does not have an assigned classroom, so he goes from room to room, class to class, pushing his apparatus and his books with him in the cart. Patuleia leans toward Murphy. "You've got a problem in one of your morning classes," he tells Murphy. "A problem? What kind of problem?" Murphy asks, thinking to himself: A knife problem? A gun problem? "I can't tell you exactly. But it's two of your students. You have to separate them." "Which two?" "I can't tell you that yet. But I suggest you rearrange the seating in your classes. Tell the students you do this at the start of the fourth quarter of each year, and just shuffle them. This problem will go away if these kids are moved apart." Murphy is puzzled. A student comes tearing around the corner and runs past Murphy and Patuleia, into the stairway and down the stairs. "Excuse me," Patuleia says, and runs after the kid.

"I love this job," Patuleia later says. "This is not work to me. Sitting behind a desk adding up numbers, that would be work. But this—" he gestures toward the teeming halls—"this is not work. This is life. I like living this life. It's 110 percent. I like the need to get things done, the real-life tests of what you plan and what you execute. Even the running from place to place, even the chasing around after the kids. This to me is the life I live with great satisfaction."

Bill Murphy is not satisfied, though, and seeks Patuleia out later in the day. Patuleia says he can't tell Murphy all that he wants to tell him—something to do with the parents of one girl. But he tells him the name of the students, two girls. Something happened outside of school, a parent was hysterical, the girls needed some distance from each other. That's all. Murphy is relieved. He didn't want to shuffle his students, and he particularly didn't want to lie about shuffling the seats every fourth quarter. "This is a crazy school," Murphy says, "and it's getting crazier."

Later that day, Murphy has another unexpected meeting, this one with the vice-principal responsible for discipline—the man with the framed picture of Hubert Humphrey on his wall. He comes into the classroom while Murphy is teaching and calls Murphy into a huddle around the desk at the front of the room, strewn with magazines and maps and open texts. "What was your problem with Sandy yesterday," he asks Murphy. "Well, he told another kid to fuck off in class," Murphy says. "Oh he did, did he?" the vice-principal says as he straightens up and turns to face the students, all intently listening. "Then I've got no choice—I'll throw him the fuck out of here. Come with me, sir," he says, pointing to Sandy, and out they go together.

"Now, I don't mind that the administration wants to respond to the kids who are causing trouble," Murphy says later. "Patuleia's trying, and he's 100 percent better than what we had before he came, but why do they have to interrupt my class to deal with these little things? I handled this kid, Sandy, who said what he said in my class, and I wanted nothing more than some record down in the office that I had had words with him. I didn't want a visit in the middle of my scant forty-minute class session. I didn't want him pulled out. But this happens all the time. The other day, one of the monitors came into my class in the middle of another lesson. Angie had called one of the vice-principals a woman, so she was on in-house suspension and they wanted me to write out the classwork for the day so she would do it down there in the detention room. So he's taking a chunk out of my time, and the time of thirty other students, to get this done in the middle of my lesson.

"Some teachers here like this kind of thing, though, because they don't really want to do the teaching. Instead, they want the kids out of their sight. If they could have every kid in detention, that would be ideal, and they'd just sit in an empty classroom reading their newspaper. Lots of teachers here would like that. But it's not that they're bad people, or even bad teachers. You know what it is? They're discouraged. They're disappointed. They feel let down by their students' inabilities. Even more than their behavior, it's the fact that they can't do the work they should be able to do. The students don't speak English well. They don't think quickly. They don't feel comfortable in the classroom. They don't have the general background knowledge—the information. And many, many teachers here don't know how to overcome these things. So they want the problems to go away. They'd rather come in and have bright, white faces ready to turn on and learn, to take notes and ask questions and talk and think. But if they can't have that, they don't want anything. This is not what they signed on for, and they just feel so disappointed by what the reality is today that they see no way over the obstacles. They just try to slide around them, to lay low, to wait for the end. Twelve years to go before retirement. Ten years. Eight years. Lots of clocks like that walking the halls here, keeping retirement time. Now, you look at what these kids want out of life, their career plans. How many say they want to be a professional athlete? A lot—too many. Some think about being doctors or lawyers if they're sure of their own intelligence. Lots of others think of some kind of business, some way of cracking the system, cashing in. But no one, not one, wants to be a high school teacher. And this is probably a great career for lots of these kids, kids who aren't rocket scientists, but who can think and talk and really care about what's going on in the world. Sandy, who's a joker and a pain in the butt, he'd be a great teacher—he's got the energy, he likes to move around and talk, and he's a bright guy without question.

"Why don't these kids think about teaching? Well, what are their teachers telling them? They tell them, 'Teaching sucks, I can't wait to get out, ten years to go, eight years to go, five years to go.' They tell them that teaching sucks. Now *there's* some harm being done to what these students can think about their futures.

"But what gets me the most—what really blows my mind—is the condition of the building here. Not just the little things— missing glass in the window, broken lights and blackboards— but the bathrooms, the gym. Do you know I have to wait sometimes ten minutes to use the teachers' bathroom? I stand in line, three deep sometimes, waiting. And in the gym. We require each student to take gym. If they won't do it, they fail, they can't graduate. But we have no showers for them. Ten AM, we march you around, make you lift weights, play ball—all wonderful things, things we should be doing—then we can't even let you hose yourself off, just get dressed and go back to sit thirty in a room, packed tight together. If the conditions of the building do not have an effect on you, you're comatose."

Murphy points to the wall clock in his room. "The Hiroshima clock," he calls it. There are Hiroshima clocks all over school— clocks stopped at six-ten, eleven-twenty, four-forty. Any time but the right time. "Just like Hiroshima," Murphy says. "These clocks were just ticking along, and then some tragedy struck, something so profound that the clocks lost their capacity to mark time, and the moment of that tragedy stays fixed forever. And we get to contemplate that every time we glance upward to see what time it is." In the main entrance to the school, a hanging lobby clock, square with a large timepiece in each side, keeps the time perfectly. Across the clockface that looks toward the front doors is written "Class of 1955." The lobby clock was the class gift. Just like the "city of firsts" campaign that reminds Lynners of how important their town was in 1860 and 1920, the big lobby clock seems to be saying something about the ability of the class of 1955 to do what everyone stuck in the building today, in 1994, can't quite manage.

On the second floor, directly above the main entrance, is another lobby clock, this one inscribed "Class of 1978." Three of its faces are stopped, but one offers the right time. Some suggestion about the nature of progress—from 1955 to 1978 to 1994—seems to reveal itself in these clocks, and Bill Murphy takes the hint. "We're losing ground. Rapidly. Something has got to change."

There is indeed hope for Murphy, and for the physical structure that is Lynn English High School, opened for business in AD 1930, as a plaque near the first-floor clock commemorates. Partly as a result of the shootings at Classical High, local politicians gathered the energy to push through a $7-million special bond issue that would in turn free up $70 million in state and federal funds. About half that money will go to putting up an entirely new building for Classical, an opportunity for that school to "start over," as a few observers have suggested. The rest will be spread among the other public school buildings in Lynn, including over $15 million for renovations at English High.

A few days before the vote, Patuleia addressed the English faculty and urged them to do everything they possibly could to turn out voters to support the bond issue, making it clear that English needed the physical improvements and, perhaps more important, it needed the good feelings that a winning vote would bring. Failing that, the spirit of the school would continue to spiral down along with its physical plant. On the day of the election, 16 percent of the eligible voters of Lynn turned out, and by the thinnest of margins the bond issue passed.

"Being a high school teacher in this building is starting to seem a little less like a Greek tragedy these days," one long-time Lynn English veteran offered. "Now let's see if Patuleia can spend this money the right way." Earlier, this teacher, a man with seldom a good word to say about Patuleia, told me that he thought he saw a glimmer of humanity in the new principal after all. "He had a meeting the other day, talking about the problems with the plumbing in the building. He didn't really tell us much that we didn't know, but for the first time he let down his guard, he dropped his professional-principal garbage and just told us that it was driving him nuts that nothing worked right in the school. Now that's what we needed to hear, because with a stiff upper lip he can't do anything. He probably can't do anything anyway, but at least for him to let us know he feels it, he feels the pressure of all this nonsense, it matters. We can feel like we're on the same side here, then. All the time, I see him in the hall, I'm asking myself, 'Isn't all this crap bothering you?' Because it's sure as fuck bothering us. And now there's more and more pressure on us for more student performance, more teacher performance, a lot of it from the man himself right there, and it's not all crap, we know that, but how can you do it if you're busy fixing the goddamn toilet every day? If he can show us that he knows it, that he now sees there are some problems here he won't solve, we won't solve, but that we just have to live with together, well that's a step in the right direction, that's a sign that his initiation is almost over and maybe he'll come to understand us a little better when he feels more of the frustration that we've all been feeling here for years. That's all we've been asking, all we've been thinking: understand us first, before you try to change us too much, before you start demanding more and more and more from us. Hey, we can give more, but don't suggest we've just been lazy. There's much more than that at work here, and the man is starting to figure it out. So welcome to English."

Patuleia won't be able to begin spending the renovation money for months, perhaps not even for a year or so, and once the spending process actually does begin contracts will have to be bid out, approvals by committees and boards will need to be arranged, and the collective work of making something good happen for the school will without doubt try everyone's patience and add new degrees of conflict to life at English High. But no one doubts that the strife of spending millions will be well worth enduring. Things can only get better for the sixty-four-year-old building.

One big reason the bond issue passed was the Lynn mayoral race earlier in the year. Back then, all the candidates agreed that education was a central issue. They talked constantly about the need to spend more on public schools, and when the bond issue came up for vote, enough citizens remembered their rhetoric to make something real out of it.

At first, the mayor's race had seemed like an easy test for the incumbent, Patrick J. McManus. Nearing the end of his first two-year term, McManus impressed most voters as competent and likable. He had already managed to trim taxes a tiny bit. Schools like Lynn English were clearly becoming safer, and the economy generally was starting to improve. Perhaps most important of all, two weeks before the election, McManus announced that he would add thirty-one new police to the 160-officer force. His principal opponent, City Councillor Joseph Scanlon, was known as a technocrat, a number cruncher. He lacked charisma, and his professional training as an accountant was all too obvious; he liked to stand in front of crowds of voters and talk about budget configurations.

A week before the preliminary election that would narrow the field of six announced candidates to the two top vote-getters, who would then go head to head in the final election in November, all the candidates met in a debate over education. Mayor McManus led off, proudly listing his successes—strong new principals in three city schools; less violence in the school buildings; a new alternative program for high school dropouts; and new programs for gifted students. City Councillor Scanlon criticized the mayor for buying decorative banners to hang along downtown streets. The money would have been better spent on schools, he said. Little things like the banners added up, and all that wasted money could really make a difference.

Then a local attorney, continuing his habit of always running for public office and always losing, said McManus was wrong to approve the hall monitors at English, but he didn't say why. Also, he wanted students tested for AIDS.

One of the two women running for mayor said that she would impose a dress-code in the schools, to boost morale and orderliness. She also said that immigrant families who did not speak English should be made to pay for the extra school costs of teaching their children the language. The other woman, a business owner, talked about the ways that generous treatment of local businesses—lower taxes, easier zoning requirements—can improve schools. Another candidate, the executive director for secondary education in the Lynn school system, left right after the start of the debate to go to a fundraising dinner.

Mayor McManus finished the debate feeling good; none of his challengers had looked terribly attractive. Nevertheless, over the next few weeks the mayor continued to raise and spend $75,000, while his only serious opponent, Joseph Scanlon, spent only $10,000.

So it was quite a shock to the mayor when he lost the preliminary election to Scanlon. He came in second, which meant he would go to the runoff election anyway, but suddenly everyone following the race in Lynn had something new to think about: what had McManus done wrong? No one could figure it out.

Nevertheless, McManus had a plan. He would go after the sizable chunk of votes that the third-place candidate, the school administrator, had drawn. Over the next four weeks, education would be *the* issue. McManus would hammer away at the crowds, telling them again and again all the things he had been doing right for the Lynn schools, and if he was lucky, Scanlon would keep talking about the street banners.

Articles in the *Item* with titles like "What About Our Schools?" kept track of the candidates' every word about education, and McManus ran a nice-looking ad featuring the mayor himself in a suit and tie sitting in a tiny chair, reading to a schoolroom full of fascinated white, black, and brown children. Above the photo: "Every Picture Tells a Story." Below it: "Mayor McManus Cares About Lynn's Future."

Then, two days before the election, the Lynn Police Association—the officers' labor union—had a stack of handbills printed up listing all the things they thought McManus had done wrong. The handbills didn't say "Vote for Scanlon," but they might just as well have—they made McManus look bad, and in the hands of voters, they would raise doubts about how effectively the mayor could lead his police force, an important issue in a town with the kind of crime that plagues Lynn. "We are in no way attempting to influence anyone's vote," a Police Association spokesman said, though he did tell an *Item* reporter, "Timing is everything." McManus was genuinely puzzled by the handbill. He had signed a generous contract with the police union a few months earlier, and just days before he had announced the thirty-one new officers to be hired. What was their beef? He met with the association's leaders privately, and found that they were concerned with one particular officer who had missed out on a promotion to a top position in the department. In private, McManus made a deal, and the hand-bills weren't circulated, though the newspaper played up the story on their front page. Two days later, McManus beat Scanlon by a small margin.

The same day, Lynn elected its first black city councillor ever. Matt Wills, an engineer who graduated from segregated public schools in Maryland, forced Lynn politicians to see the obvious: more and more black people in Lynn will be voting with every new election cycle; more and more Hispanic and Asian people in Lynn will vote, too. Because of this, every-thing in Lynn politics will change.

For the moment, though, Mayor McManus had a new two-year lease on his office, and in those two years, he could start to figure out how to serve all those new black and Hispanic and Asian voters. As a first step, McManus pushed hard for the new bond issue for the schools, schools that would soon be mostly black, Hispanic, and Asian. White families in Lynn are getting older—they tend to be in Lynn because they always were in Lynn. Very few new white families move into town, but lots of new immigrant families arrive every week—families from Haiti, from the Dominican Republic, from Central America. Lynn draws them with cheap housing and good public transit into Boston. To reach white voters, a politician in Lynn needs to talk about senior citizens' issues. To reach black and His-panic voters, a politician needs to talk about schools. And if McManus is to make a career as a minority mayor—a white mayor in a town without a white majority—he's got to work overtime to serve those very "minorities" who send their chil-dren to school in Lynn. So Lynn found itself with a mayor who was in love with the new bond issue idea, and soon enough, the bond issue came through.

English High's three-story structure looks a bit like a rect-angle missing one of its long sides. Inside the hollow sits a separate two-story building joined by corridors to the lower floors of the main building. The lower level of this smaller structure is the school's cafeteria; the upper level is the gym. Plans for the new bond money include building a new cafete-ria and a new gym, and converting the current space into more classrooms, perhaps wired for computers. If this comes to pass, there will be at least one notable casualty: the wall-art along the second-floor hallway leading to the gym.

The English High teams are called the Bulldogs, and heading towards the gym from the central stairway's second-floor landing, one is struck first by the growling face of a bug-eyed bulldog, bloody teeth bared, studded collar straining against the bulging arteries and muscled neck of the beast. One side wall blares out in three-foot-high letters, BEWARE THE DAWGS! Nearby, sport scenes spill over most of the wall surface. Small figures crowd around a painted football field, leaping and tackling and running for touchdowns, wearing little helmets, painted with cute pudginess and all looking like they're about to giggle. Some are brown-skinned, but most are white. Painted next to the little football field is a tennis court, with more little players jumping and swinging their rackets. The busiest scene is the gymnastics mural—hundreds of these earnest little people twisting and leaping and flipping and falling. The murals are signed "Class of 1983."

Eleven years later, there is no longer a single real-life gymnastic apparatus to be found in the gym, and the happy little people on the wall don't seem to describe the real students at English High well at all. With this in mind, a group of seniors has set out to add some new murals as their senior project. They paint the names of sports in tall red letters, and stark black-and-white images below. A four-foot-high baseball painted in relief, only its black stitches standing out, smacks into a section of a baseball bat; half a massive soccer ball, all black and white cross-patches, leans against the red letters, SOCCER, painted vertically from the top of the wall to the floor. And, most striking in its contrast to the little people from 1983, under red letters spelling out TRACK, a long black figure breaks through a red and white tape, coming over a finish line. The figure stands more than seven feet, lean to the point of looking a bit skeletal, and faceless—the head, like the rest of the body, is represented in stark silhouette.

Asked whether he would consider becoming a high school teacher, Sandy laughs out loud. "I plan to play ball," he says. "Maybe have a business if I can't play ball. I'll study some business classes when I get to college, but I'm playing ball there too, no question." Sandy's an only child—"he's a real Momma's boy," his cousin David says—and his parents worry about him. They worry about him falling into crime, they worry about him neglecting his schoolwork, and they worry about the state of his soul. "They don't force me to go to church, but I know they want me to go. But they say I'll come when I'm ready. And I know I'm not ready now," he says with a smile. "Maybe one day, but I don't think so much in church terms. I think in terms of life. I do my good deeds by living my life, and I live a good life. But I can go to the other side too, see what there is, have my influence on what I find there, too. I don't have to give up living with the people I want to live with when I'm out of my house, or when I'm out of school. I don't have to pull myself out from the places I like to go. I can be anywhere, because I can do good wherever I go."

Every once in a while, the police stop Sandy when he's out late with friends. "The police know my whole family—there's maybe a hundred of us with the same name in Lynn—and they know half of us are too good to be true and the other half are no good at all. They were always good to me until I turned fourteen, then something happened, maybe the way I looked or something, they started figuring I was one of those other boys from my family, ready to steal and rob. So they stop me sometimes and hassle me, but they know I'm keeping clean. I think maybe that's why they do it, so I'm less tempted to be carrying some weed or a pistol. They *will* stop me, I know it— and they shouldn't do it, either, they have no purpose to stop me just 'cause I'm a black male from my family—but I keep it in mind. I'm always ready for them. I stay ready by staying clean."

By then end of the day, hundreds of identical small posters have popped up at English on hallway doors and walls. A thick black peace sign, centered on violet paper. Written across the top: STOP THE VIOLENCE. Across the bottom: LYNN. Within a few days, all the signs have disappeared, except one, on the principal's office door. It remains there until the end of the school year.

Before I leave the building for the day, Jay walks by. I'm not sure it's him for a moment, but then I see his unmistakable necklace—a gold dollar sign styled out of tiny cannabis-leaf shapes. His lower lip is swollen; he looks away. He says he's not in the mood to talk.

Chapter Five

Haunted House

Every student looks forward to the end of the school year. Even school kids who love their schools and hate their lives outside understand the wave of freedom that crests on the very last day of the year, the day the doors fling open and the discipline ends, the lessons end, the year is over and time leaves its measured and metered track of weeks and terms and grading periods.

English High seniors end their classes three weeks before the rest of the school, to give them time for special activities—trips and parties, mostly. Angie has to keep attending classes for an extra week, though, as part of a deal the principal works out with two teachers who want to fail her, and keep her from graduating, because of her absences during the last quarter of the year. But she makes it to the prom, and even presents some joke awards to a few teachers on behalf of the senior class. She gets her biggest laugh calling Patuleia up to the stage. "Come on up, now," she says. "Don't be so shy. You know if it was some student up here you could put in detention you'd be up here in a flash, just hopping right on up here so fast!"

Two students—both honor students, one the daughter of a former Lynn mayor—show up to the prom drunk, and are excluded from the class trip later in the week, a day at a corporate retreat with acres-wide swaths of lush green lawn, basketball and tennis courts, heated pools and dining cabanas overlooking the ocean. "You'd never guess it would be these two," one teacher says. "They're the very best kids, but I suppose they're capable of doing stupid things, too. And the rules are clear enough. They got what was coming to them, and

maybe they'll take a lesson from this." Another teacher, re-
membering his own prom, has a more cynical view. "Drinking
at the prom?" he says in a loud, comic voice. "I'm shocked!
Shocked! Where do they learn this from?" He laughs so hard,
he almost falls down.

Right after the senior trip, the girls' basketball team goes to
the regional championships with an 18-0 record for the season. Patuleia, combining his eye as a coach with his frustra-
tions as a principal, has little good to say about the coach even
with his great record. "There's one girl on the team who's winning those games. In local ball, on a girls' team, you can do
that. She's very talented, and she's got a teammate who's over
six feet tall, the tallest girl in the league. Together, they won
eighteen games. The rest of the team works reasonably hard,
but with no real guidance. The coach has been standing around
for six months watching them win without teaching them a
thing." Painfully, the girls lose in the first round of the cham-
pionship competition. Soon after, the co-captains of the team
come to Patuleia with a list of complaints about their coach.
He tells them he doesn't want to see it until they've shown it to
the coach first. "He won't take it," they say. "It's on the list—he
won't listen to what we say." Patuleia looks at the list, and talks
to the coach. He tells the coach that some parents of girls on
the team want to talk to him about the complaints, too. Once
the coach has seen the parents, he will have to come in to talk
with Patuleia, to try to figure out how to turn things around.
The girls themselves don't want the coach fired. They want
Patuleia to hire an extra person to help him out, instead. But
the next day, the coach comes in and gives Patuleia his letter
of resignation. The principal is surprised. "Don't you want to
sit down and talk about this?" he asks. The coach says no. "It's
just not worth it," he tells Patuleia. "My wife and I talked about
it. I just don't need the grief."

The next day, a Thursday, a woman from Peabody goes shopping at some of the discount shops along the Lynnway. She
drives to the shops but needs to take a bus back home; her car
has been stolen from the parking lot. It turns up in the early
hours of the next morning at Breed Junior High, one of the
schools that sends its graduates to English. Actually, it turns
up *in* Breed Junior High, square in the middle of teacher
Noreen Porter's math room. The back wall of the room is gone,

turned into a heap of rubble. The car, a 1984 Oldsmobile, sits there among scattered desks and chairs, in front of the blackboard, with a wrecked front end, buckled hood and bumpers, broken lights and torn metal body, suggesting that some kind of disaster-training instruction has just taken place and soon everything will be put back together. But the Lynn schools business manager guesses it will take about $200,000 to put everything back together, including a television set that melted after the car burst into flame. One thing that didn't melt was the brick tied to the accelerator. The police figure the culprits must have tied the brick on while the car was in park, then reached in, threw it in gear and leapt clear. They weren't caught.

Two days later, on Saturday morning, a Classical High tenth-grader walks out of her house with a friend. They've been invited to another girl's house to look at her prom dress; the prom's over, but she still wants to show it off. Along the way, the tenth-grader is hit in the leg by a stray bullet. "I didn't even know I was hit," she tells a reporter from the *Item*. "My friend said I was bleeding. I looked down and my leg was all bloody." She isn't seriously hurt. "I was just worried about my pants and my sneakers," she says.

Two boys are arrested for the shooting. It turns out that earlier in the day one of them, a 14-year-old, had run away from two others who were threatening to beat him up. He ran home for his gun, a silver pistol, and for two of his friends. Then the three of them hid in a nearby backyard and leapt out as their intended victims walked by, the 14-year-old firing away. He missed the two boys who had threatened him, but one of his bullets found the tenth-grader's leg.

If the 14-year-old shooter had done well enough in school to keep up with other boys his age, he might have been a freshman or a sophomore at English High. But he was behind. He had finished elementary school just a year ago, and then never showed up at his junior high school, Breed Junior High. "We didn't know where he was," said the Lynn truant officer. "He never surfaced all year." After the shooting, police discover that his mother has moved to Peabody, though the boy never attended school there either. Police also find an outstanding arrest warrant for the mother, for prostitution, and arrest her along with her son.

The same week, June is arrested for breaking and entering, and for drug possession.

She is arrested not in Lynn, but in Salem, near the Lynn border. It happens at "the circle," a half-mile loop of road called Clark Street on a rise up off a commercial strip. The houses on Clark Street look out over the last area of real open space for miles—a few hundred acres of scrub and rock that also shelter the Salem town dump, a golf range, a Campfire Girls campground, and a gravel quarry. Slowly, the open land is being developed, with a cluster of condominiums going up here, a strip mall going up there. Still, it's an attractive place, offering a hint of rural solitude within the semiurban sprawl that contains Lynn and Salem.

The only way to get to the circle is to drive past Pulio's Drive-In Dairy Bar on Highland Avenue, past the auto parts shops, past the discount furniture outlets, and through the parking lot of a take-out chicken place. Clark Street begins with a sharp ascent, and within a hundred yards the feeling of the street changes totally: no longer humming with traffic and commerce, up on the hill the loop of Clark Street is a small town, with about fifty families living mostly in modest homes, work-a-day pickup trucks in the driveways naming the occupants: Johnson Carpentry, Arnold and Sons Metalwork, David's Paging Services. Two short streets lead away from the main circle and end in dirt roads; from the dirt roads, a small vista opens for about half a mile—a line of pine trees ends the view there, and the sky is tight against the treetops. Just looking out at the trees makes you feel that you are high up.

June began going to the circle when she was thirteen. She and her sister and her sister's friends would drive out there, park at the end of one of the dirt roads, watch the sky. Maybe smoke. Maybe drink. "But we were always quiet. No one ever minded. We go there for the sunsets. Sometimes, to watch the rain."

The day of her arrest, June decided that she was done with school at around noon, and she and her friend Anna figured they would go up to the circle to hang out. Anna got her car, drove up to the bright red doors of Lynn English, and June got in. June said hi, and then she said hi to another girl, Jill, who surprised her in the back seat. She knew Jill, but not well. Then

they all drove up to the circle, but instead of parking at the
end of one of the small roads there, Anna parked halfway down
a long driveway leading to a small house.

"Some guys had been saying it was a haunted house. Every
time we went there, there were no cars in the driveway, and
one light was on inside, but it was always on. The same one,
like it was never turned off. Someone said some old man had
lived there, that he had killed his whole family in that house,
so now it was haunted. Well, we figured, let's go see. So this
girl Jill, who I don't really know so well, she says when the car
stops, 'let's check it out, come on.' But me and Anna said no,
we don't want to be walking around someone else's house, so
we'll just wait in the car.

"Jill walks up to the front of the house, rings the bell, knocks
on the door, and she waits. Nothing happens. So she walks
around the back of the house. Now, we're sitting in the car,
thinking that maybe she's looking in through the windows, to
see if it's haunted, if somebody lives there, or whatever. But
after a few minutes, a cop drives up the street. We knew something was wrong—then I figured out that she must have went
inside the house.

"The cop asked who was in the house, and we didn't lie or
anything. We were totally truthful and polite. Then another
cop showed up, and then another. They made us get out of the
car, and they were rude. Really nasty. One cop saw this stick
that Anna's father keeps in his car for protection. It's carved,
it says 'Pogo,' her father's nickname. The cop says, 'What's
this?' She says, 'It's my father's.' So he throws it into the woods
and says 'Oh really? Well what's Daddy going to think about
this?' We were just totally cooperative, but they were so rude."

Two officers went into the house with their guns drawn.
They found Jill with an armload of costume jewelry and a couple
of small pharmaceutical bottles. She was robbing the house.

"Now I didn't really know Jill. But I know her a lot better
since we were arrested. She told them that we all had a plan
together to rob this house. How could we have been robbing
the house, if we were in the car? If we were supposed to be the
lookouts or something, why did we just say hello to the police
when they came? Why didn't we run? What I said and what
Anna said match perfectly, because we told the truth. What

Jill said was a total lie. The police don't know this, but Jill has been arrested seventeen times before. She's used a middle name and initials, and she has two social security numbers, so there's no record under her real name, but there's no question that she's lying. I'm not a rat, though. I won't say that she's been arrested seventeen times to the police or to the court, but that's the truth of the matter."

The pills Jill was stealing were Percocets—they sell on the street for five dollars a pill. They are small pills, though, and Jill was carrying a thousand of them in her hand.

While Jill was being arrested inside the house, an officer went through Anna's car, making a lot of noise, throwing everything that wasn't bolted down out onto the street. He pointed to a purse and asked whose it was. June said it was hers. "It wasn't really mine, but I said it to protect somebody." She won't say who. The officer looked through the purse and found a bag full of marijuana. "It was just roaches," the hard-to-smoke ends of joints, June said. But it was enough. June wasn't searched—that would be done later, by a female officer—but she was handcuffed behind her back, put into a cruiser, and driven downtown to jail.

To the police and prosecutors, June, Jill and Anna look like a trio of girls deep into the local drug trade. The fact that they went to the house at high noon suggests to the police that they intended to burglarize from the start—daytime burglaries are professional burglaries. During the day, people are at work. If you want to rip someone off and you have the patience to plan, you plan to steal in the middle of the day. Why does someone have a thousand of any kind of pills, anyway? What is that, a three-year supply, if you take one every day? It doesn't add up. A more likely scenario, from the police perspective: the girls knew that the person who lived in the house was a dealer, they knew what kind of pills he had, and they set out to rip him off, to walk away with five thousand dollars' worth of his dope.

"I wanted to be a cop," June says. "I don't know why. One of my friends is an auxiliary cop in Saugus, and he's a great guy. I can tell him anything. I never told him about Johnny or the things that The Crew did because I didn't want to get them in any trouble, but I probably could have—he probably wouldn't have done anything, he's such a good guy.

"Anyway, I thought if I didn't do good with what I really wanted to do—if I couldn't make it with my own dress shop— then I'd be a cop or maybe join the military. So when I was in the police car going to the jail I asked, 'Will this go into my record?' And the cop said, 'I don't know. Why?' Then he said, 'You're a very nice girl, why'd you do this?' I said I didn't know."

At the jail, June was searched and then offered the chance to make a phone call. "I said, 'can you give me a few minutes to think?' I didn't know who to call. Later, when they came back, I just said I didn't want to." June was put into a cell alone. It was very small, with a wooden bench and a toilet. No toilet paper. "No nothing," June says. "And I had my period. I told the woman officer who searched me on the way in, but they didn't give me anything. All my things were in my pocketbook, in the car. It was very embarrassing.

"I don't know how long I was in the cell. I didn't have a watch, and I didn't ask anyone. I remember just laying on the bench, on my back. I didn't cry. I wanted to but I didn't let myself. I just didn't know what to think."

After some time, June was taken to the courthouse across the street from the police station. Anna's car had been impounded by the police, but they didn't arrest her at first. Instead, they told her to walk home. When she got there, she found a message on her answering machine saying that an arrest warrant had been issued for her, and that she should go to the police station to turn herself in. When June was let out of her cell and brought before a judge, Anna hadn't arrived yet— she was probably still walking home. Jill was there, though. "And I didn't want anything to do with her. Just nothing. I knew her as a kid I saw at lunch sometimes, but that was all. She was Anna's friend, that's why we were together that day, and it turns out she wasn't really so much of a friend of Anna's either. She was just grabbing on, looking for safety in numbers, I think. And now she's saying we knew she was going into the house. She wanted me to go with her—to peek in the windows, she said—but I said no. It was that simple."

June was arraigned and let go, pending her official court date. She was given a court-appointed lawyer, but she doesn't like him. "He's a dink. He showed up at my first court date without even reading the police report first." She's still not sure what will happen to her. Will she go to jail? Will they make a deal? "I don't know. It's not really in my hands now. I just have to wait." She's due back in court at the end of the summer, when she will plead not guilty.

June left her mother's house shortly after her arrest. "I've always had family problems—that's why I'm not living home. It has nothing to do with this. My mother didn't even know I had been arrested for a week after. I just didn't tell her."

Not many people at English High know about June's arrest either. She graduated officially a few days after her arrest, so she won't be around to become the subject of whispers and gossip. Still, though, some teachers have heard, and most are surprised. June was a leader at school, working first as a student aide for Ken Curtis when he was vice-principal, and then leading the walk-out when he was fired. Patuleia knew who she was, and expected good things from her. Other teachers liked her too.

But one teacher sees a logic behind the trouble June is now in. "Take a look at this girl's life," she says. "Now if she were my daughter, or your daughter, and this happened, it would be a crisis. There would be a throng of people at the courthouse, there would be lawyers, good lawyers, working on this. It wouldn't matter whether we could afford it or not—I'd sell my car, I'd take a loan, but I'd get a fine lawyer down there to make a deal for my girl. And I'd do it because I'd be thinking, my God, this could ruin everything—school, jobs, her whole future.

"But isn't it strange that this girl can take her arrest in stride? That there seems to be very little lost here? I mean, her whole life, her family, her aspirations, it all seems easy to bend around her arrest. Is her family upset? I don't know. She's not too close to her family, is she? She says she was moving out anyway? There you go. It doesn't matter too much to them, I guess. Her job? Is she planning to work for the government? For a major corporation? To be a doctor or a lawyer? I don't think so—she wants to own a store? Strange, that she wants something that stands so free and clear from her personal history, from a criminal record. But that's how her life is. No one ever told her to dream about the kind of success that demands you keep yourself out of trouble. No one ever held her hand and led her toward the kind of life that lets you spend your money in someone else's boutique, that lets you be a leader the way this girl can be a leader. She led a thousand kids out into the street. She could lead a thousand kids as their principal—but not if she's a convicted felon. She could lead a political movement, but it's harder with jail time behind you. She could be more successful than most of the people who were her teachers. But if she's convicted of robbery and large-quantity drug possession, some doors are going to close.

"The worst thing, though, is that she won't even know it, because she's not looking toward those doors to begin with. She's looking toward the kind of life that people in trouble can live, instead. Own a little shop. Stay out of jail. Take some drugs. That's just such a waste.

"And look at all these other kids here. You know, a student is going in the right direction if she has something to lose, if we give her enough hope that when she thinks about going to jail she says to herself, 'No, I won't let that happen, I have too much to lose if I go to jail.' Why didn't June think that? Why is it so easy for her to take this in stride? And why are so many of these kids in school living such low-profile, low-volume lives? They're getting ready for failure. They're shaping their dreams so that they can say, what the hell, a little jail time, that's nothing.

"We need something totally different. We need to start every day with telling these kids, Don't you dare go to jail! Don't you dare fail! What you do matters too much. There's too much in front of you. You're too good for that. I tell my students that every day, and I know that's doubly true for June. How dare she let this happen to her! How dare we fail to let her know how precious she is. How dare we help all these kids, these thousand kids, expect so little.

"Every day, we have to remind each student here that bigger things are coming down the pike for them, and that their job is to get ready, to stay worthy, to keep clean. Tell them there's too much at stake for this crap—'Oh I flunked tenth grade, I don't care,' or 'Jail don't mean nothing.' If jail 'don't mean nothing,' if you don't care, if it 'don't matter,' then somebody forgot to tell you something about how important you are. Here's an English lesson, ok? Because this isn't just self-esteem nonsense, this is the meaning of what we teach, of literature. Here's the lesson: Walt Whitman, the American poet, wrote, 'I contain multitudes.' What does that mean? It means that June contains a lawyer, a doctor, a judge, an attorney general. It means this scrubby young boy who can't spell his own name contains a physicist, a teacher, a good father. It means every one of these kids contains much more than they each think. I'm teaching them English today, and that's my lesson: You contain multitudes. Don't forget that. Don't go to jail. Don't hurt yourself. Good things are coming, so get ready—that's your job."

June's new boyfriend, Will, likes to take her on walks along the stone seawall at the wide beach that marks the eastern edge of the border between Lynn and Swampscott. It's a pretty place, near Lynn's nicest neighborhood. The beach is a wide horse-shoe, pulling up at its curve to Humphrey Street, a two-lane north-south artery lined with old homes on the Lynn side of the border and small shops and restaurants on the Swampscott side. "We try to go there when nobody's around," June says. "We walk, talk, hold hands. We go up on the wall at high tide. Other times we go to his house and hang out. We babysit his three-year-old brother. Just like with Chris and my brother, we play the mommy and daddy role. His brother loves me. He's totally in love."

Since her arrest, June hasn't been back to the haunted house. "They closed off the circle, up where I was arrested, since all that happened. The dirt roads are totally closed off, and they don't let parking on the street at the main circle now either. Now we don't hang out there. We have to hang out places we could get in trouble, like Revere Beach," two towns to the south, "but people always end up fighting there at night. Idiotic stupid people go there. At the circle, we could all be alone, without jerks from Revere or Boston trying to fight or pick us up or anything. We had a really safe place. We weren't getting into any trouble. We didn't have to worry. There were houses nearby."

For June, "safe" is a relative term. There is enough for her to fear that she doesn't seem to realize that others might fear her, that she and her friends—boys with guns among them, at least one murderer among them—can themselves make other people afraid.

June's new boyfriend is a quiet boy. He goes to school at the vocational high school in Lynn, studies auto mechanics, and he works at an auto shop. He doesn't want June to work over the summer; he'd rather give her money. "But I don't want to be dependent," June says. "I want my own money so I can think about Will without thinking about money." After looking for a few weeks, June finds a job in the food court at the North Shore Mall. She likes working, likes keeping busy. Still, she sleeps till noon many days, getting ready for work only slowly, not really starting her day till four, when her shift begins.

June lives now with her friend Lauren and Lauren's parents. Lauren goes out with Will's brother, and the four of them—Lauren, June, Will and his brother—are a tight circle. "When I fight with Will, Lauren comes to me and says, 'Talk with Will. You guys are so good together. Work it out.' We fight over the stupidest things. I'll be talking about an ex-boyfriend, saying to Lauren, 'Remember when we did this' or 'Remember when we did that,' and Will just gets really mad. But he's never threatened me. If he gets mad, he'll just go 'Arrr!' and hit the wall. I just go 'Arrr!' without hitting. That makes a little more sense."

Like her friend June, Angie began the summer with problems. She moved out to the Berkshires to begin a summer precollege program at North Adams State College. The school was gathering their at-risk minority students for a few weeks of extra orientation and college-level skill development classes, things like how to study, what to expect from professors, how to write a college term paper. But after three days, Angie was thrown out. She won't talk about it. Joe Patuleia takes her failure at North Adams personally, but he isn't totally surprised by it, he says. "I can imagine she started asking too many questions, 'Why do we have to learn this,' 'Why do we have to do that.' I can see it clearly.

"You know, I took Angie under my wing a little bit this year. I spent time with her, helped her smooth out some conflicts with teachers. I had faith in her. She's bright, she's got a strong personality. There's really no reason she shouldn't do good work and succeed. I'd tell her, 'You can make it, no question, but you've got to settle down a little, not get so loud so often. Just sit and listen a little more, calm yourself down.' And she did, for a while. But I made a mistake. I sent her a letter, saying I was proud of her, that she was doing great. Well, that was like the kiss of death. Right after that, she just lost it, skipping classes, mouthing off to her teachers. I'm sorry I wrote that note now."

A few weeks later, Angie manages to gain admission at Assumption College, a Catholic school in Worcester, about fifty miles west of Lynn. Assumption is a reasonably good school, not very different academically from North Adams State, though Angie will have less freedom at Assumption. Remnants of the old Catholic monasticism cling to the Assumption campus, and she'll face curfews, close supervision in her free time, and rigid expectations about her behavior. If she was too loud at North Adams, she'll have to be doubly quiet to make it at Assumption.

Joe Patuleia's summer starts off far more pleasantly than Angie's or June's. He can look back on a strong year. "I won the battles I needed to win this year," he says. "I made big strides to win over the oldtimers, and I got to put some new people into key spots." One of his vice-principals, a man who began his service under Patuleia with more invested in Patuleia's failure than his success, has finally begun to support him, after two years. "You know, when I think of how hard I worked for my principal when I was V.P. in Manchester, only now that I've been a principal myself can I understand how much the principal there must have enjoyed having me around. I really busted my hump for that guy. It was like the Lone Ranger and Tonto. I was Tonto, happy to learn from the man himself, happy to do the hard jobs for him. I wanted to be the Lone Ranger, it's true, but I was happy to be Tonto anyway."

Especially pleasing to Patuleia is the thought of the new-teacher hiring he'll be doing in the weeks to come. "This summer, I'm hiring eight new teachers. That'll give me about fifteen total that I've hired, fifteen of my people, young people, hard workers who come to the school through me, and take my vision of how the school should run as *the* vision." I ask him how the new teachers are different from the old, and he tells me what I expect to hear—they're young, they're better trained. Then he thinks for a moment, and says, with gravity, "Also, I'm trying to hire people who are not from Lynn. I'm ending the patronage machine."

Patuleia takes a deep breath and says, "This year was the year. This year we turned the corner. Now the school is moving up, and everyone who cares can see it." He points to three measures of new vitality at Lynn English. "First, school spirit is higher. The kids care more about the sports, about the name of the school in the community, and about each other. Some people can criticize and say I'm trying to make the school over as a suburban high school, that there's something wrong with that. Well, it's true, I do want this school to be more like a suburban high school. But why is that wrong? Look at what a suburban high school does. It meets the students' needs academically, socially, and in sports. That's good. These are things every kid, in the suburbs or in a city like Lynn, ought to get from their school. They should feel a strong identity with the school, they should feel proud to be part of it. That's school spirit. You can see that here now, at English. That's one way to measure success in turning this school around.

"Another way is to look at safety. This is a safer school, no question. Everyone sees that. It's in the numbers—fewer fights, fewer thefts, fewer problems overall. It doesn't mean we're immune from the serious violence. The shooting at Classical, that *could* have happened here. It strikes like lightning sometimes, any place, any time. But if there are kids in my school capable of that kind of violence, maybe I can reach them in small ways. If they feel safer in the school themselves, maybe they won't try to protect themselves with violence, maybe they won't be as likely to shoot out of insecurity. And if they see that in this school violence is punished, maybe that will have an effect, too. But it's hard to say. There's a kind of arrogance in thinking that we can stop a shooting. I can't blame the principal at Classical, no one can. You can do everything right, and still it will come to you. You do everything you can, but you know there's an element of chance. In some ways, I think of the shooting and I just say it wasn't our turn yet. It's horrible, but every principal in every high school in the country must have the same thoughts. But all that aside, we've had real success this year with safety. The school is not only safer, it's now *safe*, for the first time in a long time.

"Another measure is the support the school gets from outside. NYNEX is helping out greatly as a school partner, funding extras like the staff appreciation night and some special programs for the kids. They do it because they believe in the school, because the impression is taking hold that education in this building works, that we're working toward the right goals, and taking the students—many of them students with real problems, with real obstacles to their own success that they bring into the school with them—we're taking these kids to a higher level. And we are. Not every one, but the kids who come and look for the opportunities, we've made it a lot easier for them to be found in the last couple of years."

One student with more opportunities than he expected is Evan. In June, he increased his hours at Shaw's supermarket in Peabody, and settled in to a summer of work. But in August, an unexpected chance came up for him to spend two weeks in Chicago working in a high-tech video production center for a national insurance company.

"It wasn't a bad summer at first," he says, "but it wasn't anything really special either. What came next was taking all my thoughts. I was getting mail from Emerson College every couple of weeks, new forms to fill out for the dorm, for financial aid, for the first-year classes. That was the exciting part of the summer at first, just thinking about college. And I was happy at Shaw's because I'd worked my way up to running the frozen foods department and I was more or less my own boss, no problems with a supervisor or anything like that, I was just doing my work in the big freezer. And I was really, really happy about going to Emerson College."

Evan had visited the college video production studio right before summer vacation, and he'd been impressed. "I was amazed. Just shocked. When I walked through it the first time, it was so big, two full studios, the cameras and lights and consoles, it just blew my mind. The cameras came from the *Kate and Allie Show,* and some of the other ones were from *Regis and Kathy Lee.* It was big time. Everything was humming from the fan motors to keep the equipment cool. The whole space felt alive."

After a couple of weeks at Shaw's, Evan got a call from his aunt. "Well, she's not really my aunt. She's my grandmother's sister's daughter, and she runs the design program for this company in Chicago. She knew I was going to Emerson, and she asked the people in the video production center there if I could come out for a couple of weeks and help them out, work with them in exchange for just learning, and they said yes, so I went out."

Evan had never been in the Midwest before, and the change from Lynn's hilly New England oceanfront took him by surprise. "The whole area felt totally different, Flat. Very flat. And totally new. I stayed with my aunt in her condo in Buffalo Grove—which is the funniest name for a place I ever heard— and it just felt like the whole area was prefabricated and dropped down in empty fields. The trees were all small, the space around the buildings so open. There was just one part of town, where the churches were—you could see it was the older area, the town center. That looked like here, but every- thing else looked totally different, *felt* totally different.

"And then where I was working—it was in a cornfield. Actu- ally, it was in a golf course, but the golf course was surrounded by cornfields, and at the center of the field, just standing out against the corn, was this group of five buildings, like five or six stories high, and that was the corporate center.

"The studio where I worked made mostly training tapes for insurance agents and stuff like that. But I worked on one project that was different from the guys-in-suits stuff. It was a public service announcement the company was producing, about re- cycling. So it starts out with a little boy reciting this famous poem, you know the poem "Trees," the Joyce Kilmer poem? God, I can still see him doing it, I looked at that thing a thou- sand times. So, we set it up like he was on stage at a school play or something like that, and he's just really cute and everything saying the poem, and then, sharp cut to a corporate guy mak- ing a huge mockery out of recycling, just throwing out heaps of paper, making a million photocopies with ominous music swelling up, and then another cut, to a big nature shot, forests and rivers, and a voice-over about saving the forests, making two-sided copies, things like that. That's really the message: don't make extra copies.

"Which is really funny, because one of the things I did, work- ing with my aunt, was rushing out to Kinko's to make copies late at night when the color copier at the office broke and she needed something the next day for a meeting. So there she is, the boss, out at night making sure the copies are made. But that's part of what I went out there for, to see how that kind of business environment really is. I never heard of Kinko's before. I did a lot of things I never did before, never thought about doing. It was great.

"You know, they had these conference rooms. They were actually presentation rooms, that's what they called them, 'presentation rooms,' with huge video monitors, dark carpeting, just amazing places to see something. I was dying to get in there and watch *Star Trek*, but that didn't happen."

David found himself with a different kind of opportunity once school ended for the year. He wouldn't talk to me about it, but one of his friends did. "David, he's not working now. He *won't* work now, you know? I got him a job where I'm working, at the carwash on the Lynnway. Brushless. Just a bunch of niggers like us scrubbing, scrubbing, shining, shining. Looks real good when you roll through the end of the tunnel there, sun's bouncing off your headlights, bouncing off your tires even." He likes talking about his work. He's proud. "So I got the manager to tell me that I could bring David by, cause I knew he wasn't 'gonna go out and work himself into a sweat looking for a job, but I figured he's got to be needing some money. So I set it up, and he just said 'nah, man,' and that was it.

"Now, if he just wants to be sitting in his room all day, or out playing ball till he's so stupid he can't walk home, you know that's all right with me, man. He wants to be borrowing a couple of dollars even, that's all right too. But the minute he's buying *me* lunch, then I know he's in business." Then he knows David's selling drugs. "I can't even tell you how many kids he hangs out with who make that green money. He could just roll out of bed in the morning and make a hundred dollars so easy like that. I'm not saying he's doing it, but why won't he work with me? Not cause he don't need the money, everybody needs the money. So I'm thinking about this boy's income, you know? Says he wants to play ball all summer, that's all right with me too, but there's playing and there's playing, you know? It's a long way till next year, a lotta nights, too many chances for that boy to make a dollar, I'm thinking."

David and Sandy and Jay spend some of those nights at The Palace, a club on the border of Lynn and Saugus, not far from the area where June was arrested. Just a bit further down Route One, the businesses cluster closer together, big discount outlets crowding two-story restaurants and three-story nightclubs. After dark, the neon is almost blinding—a giant green cactus in front of one club, a blue-lit neon '57 Chevy airborne in front of another. The clubs all offer plenty to drink and plenty of parking, making the long drive back to Lynn's neighborhoods a precarious one. Most of the clubs fill up during the week with thirty-something suburbanites fighting the loneliness of the North Shore's apartment complexes, but on weekends The Palace is different, attracting the hard core from Lynn's outlaw drug trade, the hundred-dollar-bill crowd. With them come the wannabes, the younger kids trying to push through the front door with fake IDs, and trying to breathe in the insane vitality of older brothers and cousins ready to die young for a few more dollars and the drug-pump of feeling alive. It's a dangerous place to be in the summer, a place where fights and feuds that dog Lynn English through the rest of the year begin.

The music is too loud, the barrooms and dance rooms are too crowded, and the liquor is unmistakably watered. It's not a place people who know they have a choice would go, really. And so you have to wonder how the young people crowding into it like lemmings crowding toward a cliff came to think of their lives—of the warm, summer nights of their youth—in such narrow ways.

June and Will seem to know something that the sweaty young people out on Route One don't. They at least hear the ocean in their summer's free time, and they seek out quiet places. But they have done no better with the chances of their lives, really. They can point to very few who would want the little that they find themselves with, even this early in their lives.

Others in Lynn, mostly older people, worry about kids like June and Will and David. Summer is when the generations mix most, it's the season of street parties and street fights, of kids walking home from friends' houses and from jobs at two in the morning. It's noisy, sometimes it's scary, and sometimes it's dangerous. In July, a city councillor proposed a curfew for everyone under eighteen all summer. After midnight, teens could be arrested for trespassing on public property, or taken into protective custody until morning, and business owners could be fined for having people under 18 on their property after midnight. The politician who proposed the curfew called it a "youth protection" action. "The central idea behind the ordinance," he told the *Item*, "is that the city owes its youngsters protection if their families are incapable of providing it. The mayor came out in support of the curfew too, saying "We are not punishing good kids. They are either at home, or headed for home after a movie."

One English High junior laughed at the mayor's remark. "Man, maybe his kids are coming home from the movies. I'm coming home from work at midnight, or at one, maybe one-thirty." He works as a busboy at a restaurant just outside Lynn. "I don't mind if they say you can't have any outside parties after midnight, or it's a thing like you can't stay in the parks or anything—you know, like you can't do the things that are a problem. But not to be there, to ban *yourself*, instead of what you might be doing and all that—that's wrong. That cuts into my life in a hard way. Quiet streets are all right with me and all, 'cause you know I gotta be walking home myself at midnight or sometimes even later, and I'd be happy with more police around, with nobody in the shadows, you know, but this is just too much. This is just about somebody doesn't like me, so they make up a law against me. That's not right. You tell me what I'm doing that's making a problem, maybe I'll be able to deal with that. But just to say, off the streets with you, nah, that ain't right."

Others against the curfew say it's too negative—telling young people what they can't do, but giving them no alternatives, no teen centers, no place to go if they don't want to be in their homes. One local woman who wants the kids off her street at night still sees their predicament. "Look, these kids, some of them can't go back home—that's where all their problems are coming from in the first place. Give them something else, a place to have dances, to play games. Then you can tell them to get off the streets. I'll thank you for doing that myself. But this is harsh. We've got to find a way to give these kids something positive before we start telling them all the things they aren't allowed to do anymore."

Two weeks after being proposed, the curfew is passed by the city council, and goes into effect. The publicity around the debate was so intense, though, that kids began staying off the streets well before the curfew was enacted, and in the end, it was hardly enforced at all. The police chief himself never came out in favor of the curfew. He accepted it without enthusiasm or complaint, and then saw one of the quietest summers in years unfold.

The curfew shouldn't get all the credit for that calm, though. Several hundred low-income Lynn teenagers found themselves in state- and federal-funded jobs programs, and that certainly accounted for a youth population often too tired for mayhem. Different programs had young workers painting fire hydrants and mailboxes, cleaning public buildings, and clearing patches of parkland in Lynn. The sight of young people working and sweating in the sun pleased a lot of people. "They're doing the right thing with these kids," said one business owner. "Take them out to the woods, make them work their asses off all day, give them a few bucks, and then they'll go home, buy a couple of sodas from me, and go to sleep. Without this kind of thing, they'll be in here all night ripping me off, one bottle at a time, or with a gun in my face."

One 17-year-old turned his new work skills into trouble, though. After a few weeks painting public buildings for Greater Lynn Senior Services, he was seen spray-painting initials on a public transportation building in town. Police caught him late on a Saturday night, after a dramatic foot chase that ended with him being cut off downtown by a police cruiser, lights spinning, shooting out of a side street. "I heard about him," David tells me. You know what I think his problem was? He was working too hard. A boy like that got to play more ball, so those cops can't catch you." A Lynn English history teacher heard about the arrest, too, but he still supported the jobs programs. "If they catch a kid like that for graffiti, I say that's entirely good news. Catch him now, for the little things, and maybe he can learn a lesson. Don't throw him out of the program, either. The first thing you do is you take him back to that building he painted, give him a stiff wire brush, and let him spend a day scraping that paint off. Next, send him to one of the train overpasses and have him work on that, clean all the graffiti off that one too. Give him a couple of weeks of that, and he'll never want to see a spray can again. It's when a kid like that's not caught on the little things that he'll keep moving up, till somebody's laying on the sidewalk, and then he'll enter the system too late to be helped, after the harm is done. Throw him out of the jobs program for the rest of the summer, and all he'll be able to do to kill time is walk around town scaring people, thinking about how to get some money in his pocket. That's when I would worry. But with all the youth jobs this summer, I'm more relaxed than ever. Something good can happen for these kids if they have the right kind of help to keep busy. That's what I like."

For Bill Murphy, it's hard to find much to like at the start of summer. It's a bad time every year. He loves teaching, and he misses the students. And then comes the annual horror show—the summer-job search. He starts this season with an interview for the Lechmere retail chain. "They had me take a psychological profile test," he recalls soon after. "I didn't get the job. Hopefully, there wasn't a connection between the test and the lack of an offer." He chuckles, but he's not happy. His biggest problem is that people don't want to hire teachers for good jobs that open up in the summer because they know that in the fall, they'll leave. "My other alternative is to lie and say I'm looking for a permanent job, but then they've got to ask what kind of guy is this forty-seven-year-old whose ambition in life is to sell furniture?" He hoped to get a job at the Jewish Community Center in Marblehead, supervising a sports program for their day camp. He didn't get it. Then he applied for a landscaping job. He didn't get that one either. "I must have been rejected for ten jobs," he says. Then he was offered a low-wage spot at a bookstore opening up near the mall. "It was really a temporary job, but they didn't tell me that. So I worked for them unpacking boxes, and then they terminated me when the boxes were all unpacked."

He tried to get a job at a vending machine company, but they hired someone else. Then he got a position selling insurance over the telephone. He's still gathering material for the classroom—"I spoke to a woman whose husband is in a nursing home the other day, trying to sell her a policy. She's paying five thousand dollars a month to keep him there. Can you believe that? It sure says something about the need for health care reform, doesn't it? You need to know this to think seri-

ously about what the President is trying to do in Congress"—
but the money's not what he needs it to be.

So he finds an extra job, with a high-end furniture store.
Like the bookstore, they're opening a new outlet near the mall,
and even though he was hired as a salesman, Murphy starts
out unpacking boxes. "I unpacked a red leather recliner chair
with brass button tacks, a beautiful piece of furniture. But you'll
be amazed by the price—twelve hundred and fifty. This is not a
place ordinary people will shop. The old Yankees will come
in, I suppose, spending some of grandfather's legacy."

Murphy's worried that the furniture store, just like the bookstore, will fire him once the boxes are empty. But the summer's
progressing, and eventually the new school year will call him
away from the red-leather sofas, so it's a risk he can bear for
the moment. "I'm working too hard, no question about it. And
it's not the kind of work I really want to be doing.

"I'm good at teaching. I can't wait to be back in school. That's
where I belong." And if money weren't a pressing need—if
Murphy wasn't thinking about his three children, his exwife,
his rent—that's where he'd be all summer, working with his
students for little or nothing. In a strange way, though, his
struggle to stay even with his bills gives him more in common
with his students than a wealthier teacher could be. If the image of Murphy strapping a leaf-blower to his back and dusting
up a millionaire's front lawn seems odd to suburban thinkers
about the state of education—is he a teacher or a gardener?
could he possibly be both?—it is a perfectly sensible image to
the students at English High who see their parents and their
friends and too often themselves go off to menial jobs every
day.

Joe Patuleia's thinking about the new school year, almost
upon him. He's high up in the roof-level cupola in the
Marblehead house he shares with the woman in his life, a former
oil company executive studying to become a therapist. The
view is striking—crystal blue water in three direction, sails in
the Marblehead harbor, bright sun everywhere. He's pleased
with the chances he's helped to give his school. He's also
pleased with his own chances. "I've done it all now—rural, sub-
urb, and inner-city. I ran a rural high school in New Hampshire, I helped run the school in Manchester, and now I'm

pulling it off in Lynn. From here, I should have a lot of options, a lot of choices." The woman he lives with is thinking about moving to the Southwest, maybe Arizona. How soon? She's not sure. Patuleia seems to be part of her plans too; he'll have some say in making that decision, but he doesn't seem to be fighting the idea very strenuously. How does he see himself in ten years? Maybe a school superintendent? Maybe. But for now, he's fully present at English, working harder than most principals work, and making more changes than most succeed at making.

Right before the new term begins, all the principals in Lynn are given 10½ percent raises, as part of a new contract. One of the Lynn city councillors calls a press conference the next day to announce that he believes the raises were illegal, but no one takes him seriously; just more Lynn politics, more noise. The raise brings Patuleia's salary up to about what a new law school grad would make at one of Boston's big firms. It's not great money, but it's not bad, and the numbers certainly look good to Bill Murphy, who takes home about as much as a policeman, maybe a little less.

As the new term begins, Murphy decides to keep his furniture store job, to be able to give his teenage daughter a few dollars now and then, and to worry less about paying his bills. In addition to his job teaching, he signs on to work Thursdays and Fridays from four in the afternoon till eight in the evening, on Saturdays from ten AM till five, and Sundays from noon to five. He doesn't complain about the work, and only seems happy to have the chance to earn a few more dollars. But anyone who cares about public education and sees Murphy's talent in the classroom has to feel a twinge of disappointment in a society that sends a man like Murphy away from his students—students whose company, he says, he'd like from morning till night—so he can go out and make a few dollars selling sofas.

Chapter Six

Prospects

When I first walked into Lynn English High School, I was surprised by how familiar the place felt. My own high school, John Dewey High in Brooklyn, New York, had been such a different place—built in 1969, brightly colored classrooms clustered together to fight the railroad feel of old wood-paneled schools, schools like English. How could English flood my senses with such waves of remembrance? Why did I feel that this was a place I had been, and left, and was now coming to again?

It was, among other things, the smell of food: high school food, served by cafeteria ladies. It was also the trace that hundreds of teens leave behind them in the air—some pheromonal mist. It was the fact of high school itself: Brooklyn or Lynn, old building or new, my life or theirs—walking into that building, or any high school building, you'd know that this couldn't be a *visit*, but only a *return*, no matter where your own school had been, or when, or how seemingly different.

Still, those apparent differences are worth enumerating. Dewey High School had no real sports program, had only a sliver of lawned campus squeezed between train yards and acres of high-rise public housing, and saw its student body come and go mostly by subway. Teachers in Lynn call their school "inner-city," with a touch of survivor's pride, but compared to the urban intensity of postindustrial Brooklyn, inner-city Lynn still seems a small town. Most English High students walk to school, come to football and basketball games, and many come from "English families" with alumni parents, cousins, sisters and brothers. The peacefulness of the place may be gone, but a quality of innocence lingers.

Of course, that innocence is fading. Many teachers at Lynn English feel they're living through the first days of a new, bleak era in the school's history. The changes are all about a "different kind of kid" at the school—it once was a white school with a few minority students, and now it is essentially a minority school with a lot of white kids (and still an almost all-white faculty).

John Dewey High School was similar. The year I graduated, 1981, Dewey had a student body precisely 50 percent white and 50 percent black, Hispanic, and Asian. So the same swirl of different looks and accents that fills the English halls had filled the halls of Dewey as well, and that, too, struck a deep chord as I spent my first days visiting English. None of the institutions of my life since Dewey have been as perfectly integrated—none of the many neighborhoods I've lived in since, none of the companies or colleges where I've worked.

Unlike English High, Dewey had never been a white school, and non-white students didn't represent change. Still, race was a complicated issue there. Dewey's very existence grew out of the recognition in the early 1960s that schools in the North shared more with their southern cousins than anyone had wanted to admit. Martin Luther King's campaign for racial justice had swung north as early as 1964, taking up the challenge of *de facto* segregation in Detroit and Chicago and New York just as it had worked for years on ending the *de jure* segregation of Birmingham and Montgomery and Greensboro.

New York escaped the kind of wrenching battles over desegregation that cities like Boston felt far more deeply. Boston chose to bus minority students into all-white neighborhood schools, while New York set up "magnet schools" instead, each school drawing students from a wide area by offering special programs, so no one could think of it as *their* neighborhood school. Everyone is an outsider at a magnet school. There is little neighborhood pride—no one loved Dewey because they loved the zone of public housing and swamp drainage that surrounded it—but when a magnet school works, there is greater commitment to the school as a thing chosen, perhaps even a thing won, through test scores or special applications. Dewey students came from all over Brooklyn, drawn by an "experimental" program: pass/fail grades, extra-long school day, and an unusual degree of freedom for students to roam around the building on their own.

Actually, only about half of Dewey's students were there by choice. The other half were "zoned" into the school: for students who lived in the Marlboro Public Houses, it *was* the local school, and unless they opted into one of the city's other magnet high schools, inertia led them to Dewey. By this compromise—half Dewey's students drawn in by freedoms and opportunities, the other half roped in like most other high school students in the nation—Dewey defeated racial segregation. Most of the students who *chose* were white; most of the others were black.

But the white students and the black students didn't mix much. There were exceptions, but for the most part the white students saw the black students as a danger. We knew there was a lot of crime in the Marlboro houses, and every so often we heard gunshots. Once, during an all-school party on the campus, dozens of young people from Marlboro came through the school fence and within an hour many were fighting, threatening teachers, and intimidating students. Police came, arrested about a handful of them, and later reported that some had been armed.

My neighbor David and I were the only kids from my neighborhood to go to Dewey, and the trip took a little less than an hour—first a fifteen-minute walk to the train station in Brighton Beach, then the QB train to Coney Island, then the B train to the Bay 50th Street station on the margin of the Dewey campus. Or, if we were in a hurry, we could take the B21 bus—just twenty-five minutes, but it dropped us on the other side of the Marlboro houses, and we'd have to walk around the their perimeter, knees shaking.

So for all the good that the magnet-school desegregation strategy had done at Dewey—and the good was palpable, the pride in our relative success as a place where black kids and white kids learned together was real—we were not free of racial fears and racial prejudice. In some ways, the lines were drawn all the more firmly because the conflicts of race were closer at hand than they might have been in a suburban school. In the school theater program, only two or three black students joined the dozens of white students and the story was the same at the school newspapers, the music program, and in the corps of student faculty aides. And even these black students, we felt, were somehow different from the others, from the Marlboro kids. They were like *us*, which meant—without thinking, we felt this—they couldn't be like *them*.

At the time, I don't think I recognized the way this division revolved so clearly around the question of race. But I was naive. I remember, for example, a young man named Darren. Six-foot-three, heavily muscled, Darren was one of the few black students who worked with ISGA, the Independent Study Group Activities club, a mangy assortment of hangers-on to social studies teacher George Bader. The group had a vaguely political, vaguely social purpose. No one could explain it *exactly*. Sometimes we published a weekly newspaper called *Rufus T.*, short for Groucho Marx's Rufus T. Firefly character in *A Day at the Races* (Bader had a red T-shirt that said "Sure I'm a Marxist," with a big picture of Groucho on the back). Sometimes we organized dances. Sometimes we ran no-credit student-taught courses with titles like "Ecology Today" and "Social Change." But mostly we hung around the ISGA office doing little and enjoying each other's company.

Darren was soft-spoken, and his gentleness was striking. He could kick out ceiling tiles with a running start, and spent most of his out-of-school hours training in martial arts, but he was by far the kindest person among ISGA's rabble. Not long after I got to know Darren, I began having trouble with a young hood named Alan Top, one of the hopeless white kids at Dewey from the fringe Brooklyn neighborhoods of displaced dockworkers. Top and I had been in junior high together, where he had shoved me a couple of times as I passed him in the halls, and fixed me with looks of violent contempt whenever I happened to turn his way. At Dewey, he saw me occasionally and usually muttered something vicious under his breath as I passed. I was deeply afraid of him, and turned to Darren. "Do you think you might be able to threaten this guy Top for me," I asked, "just to get him to leave me alone?" Darren said no, he didn't threaten people.

Which was a reasonable enough response, as I recognized then. But thinking back on it now, I see the danger I was asking Darren to court. Top and his friends were cruel to everyone, but saved a particularly insane hatred for blacks. Astonishing that I didn't even think about Darren's identity as a black man.

I think my attitude back then reflected a common view at Dewey: race won't matter if we won't let it matter. Looking back, this view strikes me as a remarkable artifact of naive 1970s liberalism.

Teachers at English High are naive in a different way: many really seem to believe that with white kids a minority at the school, good education there is doomed. Like the coach comparing his soccer team (mostly white) to the football team (mostly black): "They're a different breed of kid," he had said. His literal meaning, perhaps unintentional, is still revealing: these white kids come from better parents, better ancestors. So the coach seems to think, and he is surely not alone.

At Dewey, no one would have said such a thing. First of all, there *was* no soccer team. In 1967 and 1968, when the plan for Dewey High was taking shape, team sports seemed too competitive to the founding faculty, and too much of a distraction from the real intellectual work of an urban school. Teachers at Dewey were also more sophisticated about the language of race. They would feel the harshness of a word like "breed." But they *might* say something like, "These kids are more motivated." Or, "These kids know how to make the most of their opportunities." I doubt they'd be thinking in terms of race, at least not consciously. But "these kids," the motivated ones, the ones taking advantage of the school's opportunities, were almost all white. There were exceptions: the black and Hispanic students who were stars, who led clubs, directed school plays and wrote for one of the several school papers. But the situation was little different from Lynn English today, where the norm for white kids is moderate success, and the norm for the black and Hispanic kids is borderline failure.

The different way of talking about race among Dewey teachers reflected a different, and a very self-conscious, philosophy. Dewey was an experimental school, opening its doors in 1969 to test the theories of liberal education that John Dewey himself had championed early in the century. Students needed more freedom during their school day, it was thought, so John Dewey High School let them have free hours in the school day when they might choose on their own to visit the biology lab, or the library, or just take a nap. The school gave them time to talk with each other without having to sneak out of a class or break other rules. And it reduced the threat of punishment for experimenting with difficult subjects or unorthodox ideas by installing a regime of pass/fail grading.

John Dewey—both the man and the school named for him—had great faith in students: let the students be more free, and their natural instinct to experiment and to learn will lead them to a better education. From Dewey's perspective, freedom had another value, too, aside from its sheer utility in helping students learn. It also made better citizens. So the school set out to teach good democratic values by becoming more of a democracy itself. Semesters were unusually short at Dewey—there were five of them, seven weeks each—to give students more chances to choose courses. And each school day was an hour and a half longer than the city school system's standard, to give students more free periods at school. To graduate on time, each student needed to take seven courses a term, but the school day included ten periods—three extra. Taking extra classes was an attractive option; students could finish school early, or finish their mandated requirements early, and then experiment with other interests in their remaining time at Dewey, just like college students. And regular classes were not the only way to fulfill requirements: DISKs—for **D**ewey **I**ndependent **S**tudy **K**its—were classes without teachers, or classmates. A student could check out a set of books on almost any academic subject and take tests over the course of the term to earn class credit.

Dewey was built for its times. Its first students included throngs of self-styled young radicals, children of the Sixties. Among them mingled quiet sons and daughters of Brooklyn, and the youth of a then—still-hopeful Marlboro community (which would slide into hopelessness through the decade of the 1970s). Each year, more and more students chose to attend Dewey, and though the school had been designed for 1,200 students, by the time I enrolled there ten years after its founding, almost three thousand were squeezed in. But the overcrowding wasn't much of an issue, at least not for me and my friends. We were hard-core Dewey believers: sprung from the holding pens of various Brooklyn junior high schools, we could hardly believe the freedoms and respect Dewey bestowed on us. We took extra classes, began (though seldom finished) any number of DISKS, and felt at home wandering the halls of our school. No one ever asked for hall passes or yelled at us to move along into classrooms. Every period at Dewey was unscheduled time for about a quarter of the student body, so a student loafing around the halls was likely to be doing precisely what he was supposed to be doing.

These freedoms made my life livable as a high school student. They allowed me to think of myself as an individual rather than as one of a herded mass. I had the time and freedom to get to know my favorite teachers quite well, and I could take the unorthodox courses they were allowed to teach. One course, "The Kennedy Years," was an American history class that took tragedy and counterculture as its main subjects. The spring term always ended with the Kennedy Years' final class project: the outdoor Hippie Wedding. My last year at Dewey, I was one of the Hippie Grooms, and my girlfriend at the time was my Hippie Bride. To complete the effect, I had borrowed someone's cigarettes and emptied their tobacco into a small pile. Before the ceremony, I sat rolling little faux-joints, and then smoked one. I remember Larry Pero, a social studies teacher who later became principal, loudly asking "What's Peter smoking there?" and everyone laughing.

Dewey's long day and overeager students led to a proliferation of extracurricular activities. There wasn't one newspaper, there were five, including *FIREworks*, published by **F**eminists **I**nterested in **R**eaching **E**quality. In addition to the school play, students also ran a repertory theater company that offered a new round of plays every seven weeks. A cluster of political groups—mostly on the left—drew a lot of interest, and so did what must have been one of the first student groups in the country devoted to multiculturalism, called the Council for Unity. All these groups allowed students to spend unstructured time with their teachers, editing copy together for a newspaper, traveling together to events at other schools, or just sitting down together to plan for the next week or month of activities.

The single most important bit of education I got at Dewey was the regular question that Dan Friedberg, one of the newspaper advisors, would ask me and David Wagner, my fellow student-editor, every Thursday morning: "Did you read Hentoff?" Nat Hentoff had a column on the first amendment in New York's weekly *Village Voice*, and Friedberg always wanted to talk about it. So we began reading it too, and we began taking our own opinions a little more seriously.

Our newspaper, named *Vanguard* by some forgotten group of Trotskyite high schoolers, looked only a bit more serious than most before Friedberg and David Wagner got to work on it. I mostly stood by, nominally sharing responsibility, while David phoned the *New York Times* for permission to reprint maps and charts from their recent editions. Slowly, the paper went from an unexceptional wad of student newsprint with big, trivial headlines like "The Council in Action," to a smaller version of the *Times*, with articles about El Salvador on the front page. And it didn't seem out of place at Dewey. As far as we could tell, we were doing what the school encouraged—experimenting, changing things, engaging serious issues and ideas.

Like Dan Friedberg, most teachers at Dewey were happy to be there. A few had been specially recruited because of their enthusiasm for experimental learning, and their energy. Others earned a place at Dewey through years of teaching elsewhere. The public school system in New York City allows teachers to transfer from school to school based on their years of service, and more experienced teachers gravitate toward the "easier" schools, like Dewey, with higher-scoring, better-behaving students. Kind to older teachers, this system was cruel to the troubled schools and troubled students who needed the most help but tended to draw mostly inexperienced faculty. The system funneled older teachers who were looking for a few low-stress years before retirement to Dewey, even though they had little interest in the philosophy of the school. They were ballast in Dewey's experiment, holding the place down, making its reforms seem less like hope and more like indulgent inattention to the basics.

And in the long run, it was this group of old-time conservative teachers who turned the school away from its original mission, its experiment. Over the years, the rough edges of Dewey were ground down. Grades, for example, went from Pass or Fail to High Pass, Pass, Low Pass, or Fail—hardly different now from A, B, C, and F. Today, fewer experimental classes are offered; clubs and extracurricular activities are dwindling. Dewey is still a magnet school, but its draw is far less about experiment than about educational soundness. Dewey still attracts bright kids, and has kept a critical mass of serious students in an era of the New York City public schools' disintegration. Dewey can promise the chance for advanced classes in basic subjects, and its teachers are still prepared to teach ambitious students, but the school's mission has turned around. The experiment is over, its results insignificant for today's New York City students. Old-fashioned education is now the rarest commodity in the city's schools and Dewey does well today by drawing students to the promise of hard classes and no frills.

Dewey's ethnic calculus has changed, too. With many fewer white students, today's stars are more likely to be new immigrants from the Caribbean, Asia, or Central America. The metal detectors at the school's front doors will hopefully keep them safe, and many of the students themselves applaud the stiff security. The Marlboro houses are no closer than they were in 1969, or 1979, but what they represent lies closer at hand for the average Dewey student than ever before.

The fact that a school's children live in the very worlds of crime, public housing, and violence that their own teachers fear marks the new Lynn English High School just as much as it marks the new John Dewey.

Students at Lynn English like Angie and Sandy who leave English as modest success stories talk all the time about their estrangement from their teachers, their deep sense that they must make their own way out of their lives' difficulties, because these are difficulties that their teachers do not understand, and even fear. Thus Angie says Lynn English is "not a great school" even though "it's been good enough for me. I've learned what I've had to learn, no one's gotten in my way, but I can't point to anyone and say this teacher showed me something I needed to see." And Sandy says his teachers "just give it to you one time, you know—you get it the first time or you don't get it at all." Get what? He means academic lessons, but I think he also means the teachers' concern, their emotional investment in their students. They only give you one chance to prove that you're good enough for them to care about. As Sandy sees it, you either connect quickly, instinctively with your teachers at Lynn English, or you are lost to them. Sandy and most of his friends feel lost.

Does this have to do with race? Angie again: "You go to the gym, look over at the principal, see how he looks when some black kid puts the basketball in the hoop. You know he's as happy with you as he's ever gonna be. It's a high prize, it says you did enough with that ball playing, you earned your keep here at English, so don't worry."

Sandy feels pushed aside by his teachers, and Angie intuits the way it happens: he's a sportsman, "street smart" according to the soccer coach, given a place at the school that helps his teachers feel safe in his presence but does little to prepare Sandy for a life of meaningful work. Angie: "Here at this school, if you fight, the teachers and the principal, they put you on a little list, this is a bad kid, and they try to let you know, we're watching you. If you do honors classes, they put you on another list, we know you're smart, we're gonna help you go to college. If you're not serious about your classes but you're on a team, you go to practice, they put you on the list that says you may not be a smart kid, but maybe you can be trusted." And if not trusted, what? Feared?

Recall the sign hanging on Joe Patuleia's door: "Good things happen to kids who follow the rules and are kind, humble, friendly, and in control. Good things happen to kids who cooperate." Cooperate with whom? With teachers, one supposes—so this goes along with the good kid following the rules. But in control? Why? Who is afraid of these kids losing control? Again, one supposes the teachers.

It's an odd motto for a modern school—keeping kids in control—but it represents the heart of Lynn English High's challenge. It is, today, a school of mostly black, Hispanic and Asian students being taught by mostly white teachers. It is a school of mostly poor students being taught by middle-class teachers.

Like all teachers, the teachers at Lynn English must want their students to become more like them through the process of their schooling, but what if they don't? Better for the students to be at least harmless, then. In control.

But the most profound irony of this bit of sloganeering—in control, humble, follow the rules—is that outside of school other rules come to bear, other kinds of control pull at these young people. If a student learns to be in control, to be humble, to cooperate, and then finds himself among dangerous friends, what happens? Will he cooperate with them in their antisocial deeds? Does Patuleia's guidance constitute a call for conformity, for bending to the will of any leader, no matter how decent or how depraved?

Consider, again, this story Sandy told: "There were five of us. One had a gun he just got that day, one had a knife. The one with the knife said, 'Let's go do a robbery.' The one with the gun said no, so he said 'Then give up the gun, man, give it to me.' He was gonna, but I told him no, told him to forget about this guy just looking for trouble, and we walked away from it. That was my influence." Did Sandy cooperate? Was he humble and friendly? Thankfully, no.

Part of the experiment at John Dewey High School, my high school, was to see what happened when middle-class students share their public life, their school, with an equal number of really poor students. The answer: some exciting discoveries, some risk, and a lot of unstated barriers put up to protect the middle-class kids—the kids who in so many ways resembled the teachers—from the others. Today, the lines are harder to draw, because even the most talented kids at Dewey represent the scary urban culture that had not yet come to dominate Brooklyn in 1979, but which has since.

Today, you can't as easily presume that the "good" kids are the white kids and the troubled ones are black; you can't predict as easily that the theater program, the newspapers, or the honors classes will be dominated by white middle-class students, in part because there are almost no white middle-class students left at Dewey anymore.

The good news is that this new state of affairs means less privilege for the white kids, the kids who look or act in ways that send comforting social signals to their teachers. There is more equality in that sense. The bad news is that it is an equality of deprivation: all students are likely today to be treated with equal suspicion, rather than equal affection. At Dewey, this has become especially clear through the vanishing of the school's trusting, student-centered policies.

No student today could sit on the school's patch of grass smoking tobacco joints and hear only the quizzical amusement of his teacher. Drugs are a more serious business at Dewey today, as all crime is. There is no longer a nostalgic tolerance of dope-talk among the teachers, because when a Dewey student today smokes marijuana, no teacher sees his own youthful transgression—these students just don't look like their teachers any more. Instead, the typical Dewey teacher sees the jeopardy of harsher times, of a more dangerous place, even though it is the same place.

Recall what one English High teacher said after she saw her students grieve at the funeral for the Classical student killed on Valentine's Day: "In a way it's good to see this, and I don't mean this is not such a terrible thing—God, it is. But that the other students could be shocked by it is good. They feel it. They aren't used to it. That's very, very good. That they still see the value of this life, and how horrible it is that this boy is dead, I think that's important. It's reassuring to me, as their teacher, as someone who goes in every day to live and work with these young people, to know they feel all this, that they can still be moved by it." The common humanity that tragedy recalls and reaffirms is precious to this teacher in part because she cannot recognize herself in her students much of the time. They do not take the same pleasure from school that she took as a student, that she still takes at times as a teacher. They go home to a different kind of life than the life she finds inside her own front door. Their hopes are in some ways grander than hers ever were (she didn't want to be a professional ball player, or a wealthy business owner, just a teacher) and their actual prospects are far more the stuff of fantasy and tragedy (she knew she *could be* a teacher; most of her students simply cannot make a life playing ball, and most will not make a life at their own prosperous businesses). There was little drama in her hopes as a young woman, and whatever drama there was came alongside the vitality of her future, the facts of her middle-class success and the fair security of family and home and hoped-for profession. Failure, for her, meant nothing more than a bad grade. For Jay, failure means something else. He described his last brush with failure: "I thought I was gonna just snatch up on her right there, just reach out and grab her fucking neck. That's what I worry about, that I'll do that to a teacher."

There is no more bravado of transgression among the good students at Dewey today, just as there is little pride in rebellion at Lynn English, and for one reason: the danger of failure is so much greater for the average student at each school than it was fifteen or twenty years ago. Crime and drugs are not far enough away—as they were for me and my friends—to be hinted at bravely. They are close enough to feel, to fear, and to illuminate roads leading away from school. So I am not surprised when I think about Sandy's brave declarations of his good heart. He has to say these things, because the goodness of his heart is in fact undecided, and he knows it. My friends had the privilege to know they were good, and knowing that, they could act bad. It *was* an act; they knew that, and they could trust that their teachers knew it. Not so for the young people at English—for Sandy, for David, or for Angie.

A kid can't stand up to the forces of conformity and fight off the demons of normality with signs of deviance if "normal" is not part of that kid's ordinary life. My friends and I could reject an appearance of decency because we knew we were decent. But there's fear in David's eyes when he tells me about his stealing—fear that I'll see him not as a kid who does bad things, but as a bad kid. And it's a legitimate fear: in a way, David *is* a bad kid. If you saw him sprinting from your parked car with your money and radio, you'd be sure of it. He steals, and lots of kids around him steal, so for him stealing loses its power as an act of rebellion and becomes in its own way a kind of conformity. It's not a sign of rejecting the easy access to middle-class security—and vapidity—that a suburban high school student might take it for. Deviance, theft, the walk and talk of hard crime—these are not style and symbol to David, they are his nightmare. They are his likely future.

So the secret meanings of his life's objects and words are entirely different than they would have been for a typical Lynn English student years ago, probably the son of an Italian or Greek or Portuguese immigrant, probably bound for a union job that would earn him enough to buy a small suburban house. That long-past Lynner's prospect might fuel a diversion, a fast car, even a theft, a brush with the law. But the future would hover, and pull the prodigal back toward something good: "You've got so much to throw away, son, think about it." Who would say this? A cop? A teacher? "We're giving you a second chance, here, but you won't get a third." These are the clichés of concerned authority in the face of ordinary rebellion. They have almost nothing to do with real life at Lynn English High.

Sandy and Angie and David believe that they won't be offered a second chance, and that they have not even been offered much of a first chance. They have to get things right in their lives the first time around, because the cop who picks one of them up, the teacher who sees a spark of talent partly obscured by a bad attitude—these grown-ups won't be thinking about the life lessons that foolish risks sometimes teach young people. They'll be afraid, instead, like the English teacher who was terrified by Estaban Hernandez, the boy she imagined taunting her in Spanish as she passed him in the halls.

Joe, the Classical High graduate working at English as a teacher's aide, is a success story, but distinctly of the new age in Lynn. The central route marked on his behalf is not a path to follow but a spiral of failure he imagines daily, and strives to avoid. "The only fear I have is jail," Joe says when he talks about his future. As his life progresses, he does not move toward aspiration; instead, he avoids the fall.

Bill Murphy's life is the counter-example. He is the old Lynner, the Lynn English High School student who didn't become famous, didn't get rich, but kept his nose clean and found a happy life for himself. He could imagine his success early on—he knew he wanted to be a teacher, and he knew he could become one. He liked athletics and played ball well—today, nearing fifty, he has a physique to show off—but he was never deluded into thinking that professional sports was his only way out of Lynn. He never thought he'd have to become rich, maybe sell drugs, to really think of himself as a man. His world met him halfway. The rules for success were reasonable, and the means to success were close at hand: keep up with schoolwork, push through college, and there will be a modest job in your dream profession waiting for you when you're done. Not a single young person I met at Lynn English today imagines such a straightforward path in front of him or her. Most of those who do see themselves succeeding are either deluded ("I'm gonna play ball, man") or depraved ("Maybe I'll do some pimping. Ha ha.").

Actually, Bill Murphy surprised me. He had every predictive trait you'd expect a mediocre, uninspired teacher at English to have: he was a white, middle-aged townie with a degree from a local college (Franklin Pierce in southern New Hampshire). But Murphy was the single best teacher I met in Lynn, and I can't say I've met anyone more effective at any other school.

Murphy's success springs in part from sheer energy—he walks, talks and thinks quick and big. And he has a tremendous grasp of his subject: he knows American history by the book, and also by instinct. Ideas attract him, and so do the wild contradictions of American life. Call him up late at night to talk about his family, or to make a date for a drink, and he leaps upon you with the day's news: "Can you believe what's happening in Russia? Looks like we bet on the wrong horse, over there. Looks like someone named Boris is gonna take the next flight to Switzerland with a sack of U.S. aid money." And when he says, "Can you believe it," he leans on the word "believe." He really cares about what you believe, and what he himself believes. That comes through to his students as he holds up the day's newspaper and says, "Did you see this?" Like Dan Friedberg at Dewey, he sees his students not only as charges to educate, but as thinking people with whom he shares a world of ideas.

Not all of Murphy's students see this. In fact, most of them don't recognize his respect for their ideas. This is partly habit; the students have come to expect a flat performance of old material from their teachers (Sandy: "They just give it to you one time, you know—you get it the first time or you don't get it at all"), and Murphy's intellectual spontaneity is so foreign to them as to be unrecognizable. But they all feel his energy, even those who fight him, who take pride in their own flatness, their own low flickers of animation.

But many students see Murphy for precisely what he is and value him. Evan said Murphy "had that interest in what he was teaching, and in really finding out how we felt about it." And a number paid him the great compliment of repeating his own phrases back to him, showing that the ideas had penetrated (the camouflage-jacket student: "That's just a short-term solution to a long-term problem.") And he had the admiration of some of his colleagues, the men and women who suspected that they themselves could do better in the classroom if they really devoted themselves, if they had the energy to bound into the room and move around all period, every period, drawing their students out, fighting the sluggishness of their hearts and minds, but who couldn't muster the energy. Other colleagues thought Murphy just went too far, had too much going on in the classroom. "How can he think that they're gonna understand half the things he does, with those magazines pinned to his walls and the World Wars and the law," said one. "These are kids who have trouble keeping up with Oprah, most of them."

Murphy would like to have the money to take his students out of the school building, to take them hiking and mountain—climbing and walking through cities and towns they've never been in, and then have the time to sit down with them and have them talk and write about every new thing they've seen. He wants more experimental programs, more chances to put away the civic books and bring real, challenging objects into class. "I'd like to put a kayak into the middle of the room and talk about how you could live with this as your principal tool for living—for travel, for hunting, for shelter. Teach them about other ways their lives could be, radically different ways." But he gets little support and less money for these ideas. Once, after I'd been visiting English for a few days, I told Patuleia that I'd begun sitting in on some of Murphy's classes, and that I thought he was one of the most talented teachers in the building. "Talented?" he said. "Well, maybe the craziest." Like others at English, Patuleia couldn't quite get beyond Murphy's lurking threats to the status quo—Murphy's energy quietly criticizing other teachers for having too little, his wish to spend more time with students quietly criticizing other teachers' wish to get away from school as soon as they could every day, every school year, every period. Patuleia actually had more in common with Murphy than with most teachers—they both are extraordinarily dedicated educators—but he still couldn't accept the static that Murphy's very presence sent crackling through the unspoken orthodoxies of Lynn English High. If "good things happen to kids who follow the rules" in Patuleia's school, the best things seem to happen to teachers who follow the rules, too. Murphy's passion didn't quite bend the rules, but it came uncomfortably close.

I think Murphy would have been very happy at a school like John Dewey. The iconoclasm built into the place would certainly have appealed to him, and the self-selected group of students who found Dewey a refuge from the other, factory-like high schools of Brooklyn would have made him a hero. There was one course at Dewey in particular that would have been tailor-made for Murphy: The American Dream. It started in the early 1970s as a collaboration between George Bader, the social studies teacher, and Gerald Sussman, an English teacher. The original idea had been to teach history through literature, with an emphasis on popular culture and the experience of ordinary Americans at different points in the nation's history. The program quickly added a range of special events, like a mock constitutional convention, a courtroom confrontation between the South and the North to argue the merits of the Civil War, and an end-of-the-school-year rural-urban exchange, which sent us city kids to a rural high school for a week, and then had us host our counterparts in return. Bader and Sussman wound up dropping the American Dream class after a couple of years, and another social studies teacher named Lew Smith took it over, got lots of press attention for the class, and wound up writing a social studies textbook based on it. Smith had left Dewey to become a department chairman at another New York City high school by the time I arrived, though he returned to the school in my final weeks as a student to become the new principal.

Lew Smith had made some mistakes that dogged him, though, and not long after he took the reins at Dewey he was forced to step down. I've never been able to hear an official explanation of why. I had worked for Smith, along with a few other Dewey students, the summer before his return to the school as principal. We were the unskilled labor renovating a townhouse that Smith had bought in Brooklyn's most exclusive neighborhood, right at the foot of the Brooklyn Bridge and hard against the slope of Manhattan's downtown skyline. Foolish beyond any understanding, Smith paid all his student labor less than the minimum wage. We got $20 a day, about ten bucks short of what the law said we should have gotten. Later, when the city Board of Education was investigating Smith, some of my friends from the renovation job were called and grilled about Smith's pay scales. Still, some greater sin seemed to be on the school board's collective mind, though it was never spoken of publicly. Smith resigned and later turned up on local television talk shows as the director of New York's famous Lower East Side Settlement House, a social service center for new immigrants and the neighborhood poor.

As principal, Smith was at once laid back and someone to fear. Many teachers worried what his hidden agenda might be; one friendly chemistry teacher had some unspoken conflict with Smith that consumed him totally. But Smith seemed an unassuming figure, trim, bearded and smiling to himself as he walked the halls not-too-quickly, a half-reformed beatnik who had learned to work the system. But toward what end? What was it Smith was really trying to do as principal? No one quite knew. Then, after whispers and investigations, he was gone. Too smart for his own good, some said.

This no one would say about Joe Patuleia. Clearly a smart man, he seems incapable of keeping a secret, and his consuming challenge is to get a straightforward message through to the teachers and students at Lynn English, never mind secret agendas. The public agenda is hard enough.

It is an ambitious agenda, but in many ways quite conservative. Patuleia's model of a good school is the American classic: a place of order, free of violence, where students are given knowledge they do not have. As he puts it, a good school "meets the students' needs academically, socially, and in sports. That's good. These are things every kid, in the suburbs or in a city like Lynn, ought to get from their school. They should feel a strong identity with the school, they should feel proud to be part of it."

Coming from an urban, experimental school without sports, to me this model seems naive.

Should immigrant students and kids from homes in deep poverty be offered the American Classic high school? Patuleia clearly says yes. But there are reasons to say no. Chief among them is the notion that the classic education model reinforces other "classic" American ideas, especially ideas about race. Remember what Angie had to say about Patuleia: "Too many of these boys follow the bouncing ball when they should be thinking about other things. . . . You go to the gym, look over at the principal, see how he looks when some black kid puts the basketball in the hoop. You know he's as happy with you as he's ever gonna be. It's a high prize, it says you did enough with that ball playing, you earned your keep here at English, so don't worry." And Joe, the teacher's aide, who graduated from Classical High, speaking of Patuleia: "When he goes to sleep in his bed tonight and he says to himself, how am I gonna keep those angry black men away from my kids, he's never gonna find the answer to that question. He locked up the doors. . . . That's not gonna keep the angry black men out. He puts the monitors in the hall. That's not gonna keep the angry black men out either. Because they're already in. Here they are. And he can't stop a bullet in this school, or outside it. I like the man. He's working hard, and I give him respect for that. But there's only one thing that's gonna stop a bullet in this school, and that's a black man. That's a hard lesson, and I don't think he's figured that one out yet."

I see the subtlety in Joe's remark—only a black man's gonna stop a bullet. To me, that means two things: only a black man can provide the leadership that black youth in Lynn truly need to change their lives; and, more ominously, only black men will be the ones who wind up with bullets in their bodies—they are the ones who will suffer the most from violence, and from grossly inadequate educations. It is quite a statement, and Joe must feel it deeply, thinking back on his days in the boys' room at Classical, feeling the guns of other boys in their secret seclusion.

To try to find some of the substance of life for the poor in Lynn, which meant poor Hispanics, poor Asians, and poor whites, but most of all poor blacks, I set out one day to walk from my home about five miles away, through as many of the neighborhoods of Lynn as I could. At first, I felt the same good feelings familiar from walks through Harlem and the Lower East Side in New York—most of all the feeling that *this is not so bad*. These streets don't seem so dangerous; poor, yes, but not dangerous. There is life here, people on the streets, shops on the corners, crowded apartments overflowing with laundry drying in the open air, kids playing around the edges of their busy homes. Then, turning one corner, I felt sudden fear. Up against one of the many outcroppings of overgrown parkland

I came into a row of houses half-torn down, shopping carts on their sides in the streets, mangy dogs tied up in what turned out to be the front lots of decrepit small homes build behind the driveways of larger, but hardly more habitable houses—no doubt, once servants' quarters, now home to the most wretchedly poor, maybe squatters. Here was the hardest part of Lynn, and it stretched for block after block of homes that deserved to be condemned, and many probably had been, whether or not their occupants knew it, or had the spiritual resources left to care. Children live here, you could hear them, though they seemed to be out of sight, off the street for good reasons. These children, can they really be reached by Joe Patuleia's idea of school spirit?

There are alternatives. Bill Murphy dreams of an open-air school, of hard physical challenge and human attention to rewire the souls of some of these young people. ("I want to teach them spirituality," he had said, and I think of this remark again and again, "I want to take them mountain-climbing.") Stuck within the walls of a school building, Murphy still thinks of ways to get his ideas about the world across. "You know what I would do, really?" he asks me one day, over coffee in a local restaurant. "You might think this is crazy, but if I had the chance, I'd get everyone together in the morning, before homeroom, before the first class, get the whole school together in the auditorium and have them sit there and read the newspaper for an hour. Just sit there and see what's going on in the world. It wouldn't matter which one, maybe the *Herald*, the *Globe*, the *New York Times*. Some are better than others, some are maybe not quite truthful, but at least we have something to talk about then. And we can talk about so many things then that these kids just don't even hear about, that they don't even suspect are going on outside their little worlds."

Our waitress comes over to listen to Murphy. It turns out they know each other; she was a teacher at one of the Lynn junior high schools years ago when Murphy taught there, too. She'd left her teaching job after having children, and then began a cycle of teaching for a year or two and then being laid off when more senior teachers who had been on leave themselves came back into the system. "I'd like to get back in now," she says as she pours Murphy a cup of coffee, "but to start over

I'd need to work as a sub first, build up a little seniority, and then put in for a regular teaching job, but do you know what a sub gets? Fifty dollars a day. I can't take the pay cut." She gives Murphy a pat on the back and heads over to another table.

Near the end of my time visiting Lynn English, the state department of education released its own plan for shaking up schools. Called "The Massachusetts Common Core of Learning," the program offers a long list of goals—inoffensive but abstract things like "All students should read, write, and communicate effectively, read and listen critically for information, understanding and enjoyment. All students should acquire, integrate and apply essential knowledge"—and a brief addendum titled "How Can We Make the Common Core of Learning Succeed," which tries to personalize the general goals, to scale them down to particular tasks that each player in the state's education game can understand. "Students, parents, educators and our entire society," this section begins, "all share responsibility to ensure that students are in school ready to study and learn, that students recognize the importance of education throughout their lives," and so on, creating a list of about a dozen of these shared responsibilities. All neglect any sense of *how* "our entire society" is to make these honorable goals into reality, and the entire package offers little guidance to parents without much education themselves. How, for example, is a welfare mother in Lynn to ensure that her children recognize the importance of education throughout their lives? What is she to say? How does this "common core" offer her a chance to say it?

Among the other responsibilities the plan asserts, it says "Families and educators must nurture confident children, so they are able to face the challenges of a rapidly changing world." Another reality check: What is a Cambodian refugee mother in Lynn to make of this?

Bill Murphy has his own objections to the language of the Common Core. He points to another item in the list of responsibilities. "Students, parents, educators and our entire society share," according to the Core, "the responsibility to ensure that schools are models of democracy and order." "Talk about propaganda," he says. "Look at that word, 'order.'" He breaks into a mock-German accent: "'Ve must haff order!' Is there anything real in all this? Can these people imagine the lives of ordinary people in school today? Can they possibly think that they're helping? Now there's something interesting to talk about here—the way they put 'democracy' and 'order' in the same sentence. Do these two ideals sometimes contradict? Well, yes they do. Should we talk to students about that? Should we talk about the problems and challenges here, instead of this official sheet that seems to assume everything's all right, all contradictions taken care of? Where's the thinking here? Where's the admission that big issues in how we think of our society are all caught up in school reform? The impression I get reading this is that some guys in suits have done all the thinking about school reform for us, and figured it all out. Wouldn't you think that? Wouldn't most students? And that's a big problem, from where I sit."

Copies of the pamphlet version of the Common Core have been popping up in Dunkin Donuts shops around Boston, as well as libraries and schools. There are other guidelines that come with the new Common Core, kept out of the donut shops but circulated among teachers and principals, mandating a minimum amount of class time on core subjects. "But they won't include field trips," Murphy complains. "I'm taking the kids to the Museum of Fine Arts, and later to the battleship in the Boston Harbor, to teach about the Second World War, and the core says I have to sit them in class instead and show a filmstrip or something. That's nuts." English comes up short 22 minutes of core instruction a day under the new regime, and Patuleia has to find a way to add the time. He's thinking about starting the school day earlier, at 7:45, but most teachers don't like the idea. The students come in half-asleep already, they point out. Lunch is already only half an hour. They might run the day longer, but many students go to work right after school, and a handful of teachers run off to second jobs themselves, so for the moment the challenge of the core remains unresolved, and English quietly fails to comply with its standards.

The failure of the new Core to change English is not surprising. Many, many plans for change have come and gone. There was, for example, the former vice-principal's plan: "I proposed setting up three different schools inside English," he recalled for me. "On the third floor, we would run a college prep school. On the second floor, a business school. On the first floor, a school for immigrants. The immigrants could see the others, and they could participate in the other activities as they became able to, but they wouldn't just be thrown in to fail as they are now."

More than one of the former vice-principal's colleagues saw this as a kind of apartheid education, though his motives were certainly benign, and his perception of English High's failings by no means inaccurate. Patuleia's goal to remedy those failings by refashioning English as a suburban, sport-oriented, spirit-filled school can only go so far. Yet he's made English safer, and given the teaching staff a sense of stability. But what is the next step, and how ambitious should his hopes, and the hopes of the students at English, be?

The politicians of Lynn—all but one of them white, every one representing the old ethnic blocs of Italian, Portuguese, Greek and Irish neighborhoods—have their fingers in the wind and call for more basics. Patuleia seems a good steward to bring English as close to the ideal of a back-to-basics high school as it will ever get, but the politicians have no stake in the school's long-term burden of educating the new Lynners—nonwhite by a vast majority and unconnected to the political world of old Lynn—for full citizenship. The current crop of politicians benefit when the new immigrants don't vote; they benefit from the perception among remaining white Lynners that nonwhites should be feared. But their future is certain: eventually, there will be no place for the white political clubhouse in Lynn, and they will be replaced by men and women of color who will inevitably represent the city in a different way. But what way is that? Will different politicians make for different kinds of schools? Chances are they will seek school leaders who share their own heritage, just as the white men running the town tend to choose white men to run the schools. If so, Joe the teacher aide will find his words prophetic. Then black men, and black women, will have their chance to stop the bullets in Lynn's schools.

That change will, in some ways, be good. And I believe that change is absolutely necessary. I would still like to think with the innocence I held in my heart as a John Dewey High student and say that race does not matter, ethnicity does not matter. And I'm not entirely sure that race really exists. Is there a reasonable way to define the difference between black people and white people that won't wind up putting some people we recognize as black in the white category, and people we recognize as white in the black category? Any standard—skin tone, region of ancestors' origin—will wind up failing to really confirm the divisions that we have created among ourselves and which we call the divisions of race. But even if race doesn't exist, rac*ism* certainly does. And it is racism that will continue to warp the lines of communication between teachers and students at English High if it remains a school full of black and Hispanic and Asian students taught by a staff of white people. The small gestures, the tiniest differences will breed mistrust. The harsh words parents speak at the dinner table about one group, the ugly joke a teacher slips out in a bar—these things will lie in the darker corners of everyone's minds and they will continue to offer not only obstacles but also excuses that fail to explain what they pretend to explain, and fail to help anyone.

English will be a better school when more black, Hispanic and Asian teachers teach there, and this will probably not happen for years and years. Joe Patuleia's effects on the school will continue, and will be to the good. He will keep the place safer and more decent than it might be with another man or woman at the helm. And Bill Murphy will continue to radiate energy and will surely save a few students every year from giving up on themselves. But neither will be able to overcome the divisions all around us. Neither will cease to be white, their students will not cease to be black and Hispanic and Asian, and for all the terrible reasons we can list, these facts will leave the school looking more like a plantation than a place where poor young people of color learn to master their own lives.

This is ugly, but true. It describes the effects of racial division and racism in our culture. The great irony of racial reform, of course, is that many of the teachers of color who eventually take their roles at Lynn English will not be extraordinary teachers. Certainly some of them, like a similar number of white teachers, will not even be particularly good at their jobs. But because they will share important parts of the cultural identities of their students, something will happen between them and their charges that even the most visionary white teacher often cannot make happen. I hate saying this, but I think it is true.

I was amazed, for example, by Jane Turner, English High's only black woman teacher. Grady had told me how much she cared for him, how good a teacher she was. "She helps me more than any white teacher ever helped me," he said. But in the classroom, Turner was slow and petty, ready to pick meaningless fights with her students, and quick to make light of her Hispanic student's culture. "You see," she told the girl, "I know your own language better than you do." To my mind, Turner was the classic bored teacher—unexcited, intellectually lazy, doing little good and at times some harm. So why did Grady cherish her so?

Certainly she might have given him special attention that he craved, might have offered him concern and care that was not evident in the class I observed. But I think it is something more than that. I think Grady could take more meaning from his relationship with Turner because Turner, like Grady, is black. I don't mean to suggest that there is anything about being black that makes a teacher better or worse, but that for Grady and, I suspect, for many other black students, in an environment like Lynn English where virtually every authority figure is white and some of them subtly racist, a relationship with a black teacher takes on special significance. Defenses go down, fearfulness eases. Trust, even a naive or misguided trust, allows deeper communication, and sometimes deeper learning. If Grady assumed a degree of trust with all his teachers, I suspect he'd have little reason to think Turner was at all extraordinary. But Grady's race-consciousness affects his view of his teachers, just as the race-consciousness of many teachers affects the way they view their students at English.

Now, in some ways, Grady is simply wrong to react to his teacher's race. As his education continues to unfold, he will find many black teachers who cannot help him, and many white teachers who can aid him extraordinarily well. But there is an element of self-protection in his outlook. His unreasonable feelings about race reflect the unreasonable situation he finds himself in, and might indeed serve to protect him from some of the teachers at English who, like the soccer coach, might suggest he cultivate his street smarts rather than his abilities in biology and calculus.

Grady's view in many ways resembles the view of teachers at Lynn English who think wistfully of the days their students came to school with a better attitude and all spoke the same language, both metaphorically and literally. What is Grady wishing for? For his teachers to look more like him, to appear to come from the same place, to speak the same language. School should teach him that his intellect holds undiscovered qualities, and gives him an unalterable fellowship with all thinking people. But this lesson has not made it through the din of noise at English, and is not likely to. Grady still thinks he'll be a professional ballplayer, like many other young black men at English. I've never seen him play ball, but I am certain he will not make it. I sat with him once and asked him if he was the best player at English. Like a half dozen others at English, Grady is sure that he is indeed the very best. And the very best in Lynn? Well, he doesn't want to brag, but maybe. And in the state? Well, probably not the state, but maybe the top ten in the state. "So if you're right, that means you're one of the five hundred best high school players in the country right now. Is being one of the top five hundred of a single year's players good enough to be a pro?"

He saw my point but would not accept it. Without anger, he told me I was wrong. I asked him to come to my house that Sunday, so I could give him a college entrance exam study guide. I would try to convince him to come every weekend to work with me on his verbal and math skills, to prepare for the test. That's the way out, I told him, to make it on the test. But he didn't come, which didn't surprise me. He didn't trust me, and he explained why on another occasion, when I was talking to him and to David about their plans for an upcoming weekend. They were heading to a party. I asked if I could come along, to try to learn more about them and their friends for my book. They laughed, really delighted by my ridiculous request. "No offense man," Grady said, "But the Pillsbury Dough Boy won't make it, you know?" Dough Boy? It was a shot at my waistline, and maybe at my age—I would stand out as a little too old, a little too spread out at the middle. But more than that, I think he was talking about some intense quality of whiteness I'd radiate among his friends. They'd think I was a cop, he said. They'd know I was out of place. But what, then, *is* Grady's place? Is it at school? It should be—he's a young man, seventeen, a student, a bright kid.

But school's *not* his place. He feels it: it's Patuleia's place, Murphy's place, the place of coaches and vice-principals who all must seem pasty-faced to him at times. Hubert Humphrey hanging on the vice-principal's wall—even Hubert belongs in a way that Grady feels he does not. Jane Turner is an exception, even if she's not an exceptional teacher by my standards. She's a sign that something's happening at that school that Grady might recognize, that might be consonant with his own family, his friends, his private life. A boundary is crossed through Turner's presence, it helps students like Grady, helps them deeply.

Clearly, though, it is not enough. I say this because it has not yet changed Grady's dreams, the dreams of ballplaying. He has not yet come to see that there is a place for him at English as a teacher, as one of the people who could reach the younger brothers and sisters and cousins of his neighborhood, the children just being born who will look to whatever Grady does as a model of manhood, and since he is an African American man, they will see it as a model of African American manhood particularly.

Who will that model be? A neighborhood guy who wanted to play ball? Or, maybe, a teacher? Grady does not yet hope that for himself. It is my hope for him, though. Perhaps it is Jane Turner's. Best of all, it might be Joe Patuleia's. Because if the principal hopes for it, then the young man five years older, come calling to look for a teaching job having followed his better instincts, having followed the better hopes of his favorite teacher, and having followed the rules just like Bill Murphy followed the rules and became what he had wished to become— if Patuleia *hopes* for this man to walk in and ask to become the future of English High, then it might just happen. But if he does not, if in his power to hire whom he chooses he just doesn't feel this young man has what it takes, then nothing will have been gained through the leap of faith that Grady might still be convinced to take: the leap of faith equally in himself and in men like Patuleia. What an odd pair they make, Grady and Patuleia, more tightly bound together than either seems to realize.

Studies in the Postmodern Theory of Education

General Editors
Joe L. Kincheloe & Shirley R. Steinberg

Counterpoints publishes the most compelling and imaginative books being written in education today. Grounded on the theoretical advances in criticalism, feminism and postmodernism in the last two decades of the twentieth century, Counterpoints engages the meaning of these innovations in various forms of educational expression. Committed to the proposition that theoretical literature should be accessible to a variety of audiences, the series insists that its authors avoid esoteric and jargonistic languages that transform educational scholarship into an elite discourse for the initiated. Scholarly work matters only to the degree it affects consciousness and practice at multiple sites. Counterpoints' editorial policy is based on these principles and the ability of scholars to break new ground, to open new conversations, to go where educators have never gone before.

For additional information about this series or for the submission of manuscripts, please contact:

Joe L. Kincheloe & Shirley R. Steinberg
637 West Foster Avenue
State College, PA 16801